JACK URWIN

SURVIVING MODERN MASCULINITY

MAN UP

ICON

Published in the UK in 2016
by Icon Books Ltd, Omnibus Business Centre,
39–41 North Road, London N7 9DP
email: info@iconbooks.com
www.iconbooks.com

Sold in the UK, Europe and Asia
by Faber & Faber Ltd, Bloomsbury House,
74–77 Great Russell Street,
London WC1B 3DA or their agents

Distributed in the UK, Europe and Asia
by Grantham Book Services,
Trent Road, Grantham NG31 7XQ

Distributed in Australia and New Zealand
by Allen & Unwin Pty Ltd,
PO Box 8500, 83 Alexander Street,
Crows Nest, NSW 2065

Distributed in South Africa
by Jonathan Ball, Office B4, The District,
41 Sir Lowry Road, Woodstock 7925

Distributed in India
by Penguin Books India,
7th Floor, Infinity Tower – C, DLF Cyber City,
Gurgaon 122002, Haryana

ISBN: 978-178578-069-1

Typeset in DIN by Marie Doherty

Printed and bound in the UK by Clays Ltd, St Ives plc

Contents

Introduction

He was fucking with me, I am sure of it. 13 years of analysing the final words I heard my father speak, and I have no doubt whatsoever that those two syllables were delivered with the same black sarcasm as every other sentence to ever pass his lips. The bastard. The brilliant, awful bastard.

Like that of most dads, Richard Urwin's sense of humour was an acquired taste. Sometimes, the depth and complexity of his jokes would reveal the brain of a one-time Mensa member (he was too tight to renew his subs after the first year); other times, they'd eschew any sort of wit or taste whatsoever and you were left questioning in what society this man's IQ could be perceived as being above average. My brother and sister recall an incident in which our dad timed how long the extractor fan in the bathroom would run for after the light was turned off, calling them upstairs and clicking his fingers at the exact moment it stopped, expecting them to be impressed at his ability to command power over household appliances or, at the very least, for waiting seven minutes to determine the length, and a further seven minutes to execute the prank. If he'd known he wouldn't make it to his 52nd birthday, maybe he wouldn't have wasted fourteen minutes of his life waiting for a fan to turn off (oh, who am I kidding, he absolutely would have).

Much to our horror, he regularly wore tight Lycra cycling shorts; a curiosity, for in none of our lifetimes did we ever see him ride a bike. A family friend once remarked: 'I never know where to look when Richard wears cycling shorts.' In all probability, the appeal of the shorts, like the bathroom fan, like so much of my dad's personality, centred on the one thing he loved doing more than anything else: fucking with people. Such was the man's commitment to insincerity, when I asked how he was feeling after a few days off work with the flu, he stood up, proclaimed 'Better!' and made his way to the bathroom to die.

It's possible he had no idea that in a matter of seconds he'd be slumped unconscious beside the toilet. It's possible he lied in order to protect me. But the final explanation, and the one I choose to believe, is that he knew he was dying and was determined to get one last shot in. And I respect that a hell of a lot. It gives me an odd sort of comfort to think that as his vision faded and his lips turned blue, my father's final thought before submitting to the cold grip of extinction was a gleeful: 'Hahaha! I got you, you little shit!' I think he would have enjoyed that.

Three weeks later, I celebrated my 10th birthday (I got a new bike, I ate some cake, I did all the normal things you do when you hit double figures). A few months after that, I took home the title of 'funniest pupil' in a classroom awards ceremony, something which previously would've seemed impossible given my strait-laced, hard-working, borderline-teacher's-pet attitude to school. Deflecting my grief into something that made others laugh felt much better than breaking down crying several times a day – which, in reality, was what I wanted and probably needed to do. It's hard to deal with that sort of trauma in a healthy way, though: especially if it's your first real taste of what a shitty world this can be. You latch onto any kind of positivity after something so painful, and I suppose for me this manifested itself in the laughter of my peers, something I found validated me and gave me some purpose. Plus, let's face it, no one wants to be the kid constantly crying about their dead dad; a total fucking buzzkill.

When the coroner was finished rooting around inside the vessel that had, for 51 years, housed my father, a fatal heart attack was recorded, and off went dad to his fiery conclusion in the Loughborough crematorium. The post-mortem, however, also revealed significant scar tissue indicative of a previous attack sometime in the months or years previously, which was news to us all. Shortly afterwards, my mum found over-the-counter angina medication in the pocket of one his jackets, so it was clear he knew *something* was up, but apparently chest pains which had been nearly-deadly once before weren't something that he deemed worthy of professional consultation. Classic Dad!

After he died, jokes took preference over sincerity in almost any situation for me, because the idea of picking at wounds and revealing the fragile human beneath was about the most terrifying thing I could comprehend. It's a trait I now recognise as one of my father's greatest flaws, ultimately contributing to his downfall. It's also an inherent characteristic of so many men, and it's this which gave me my first inspiration for what you're reading today.

The stubborn lost-bloke-refusing-to-ask-for-directions might be a handy caricature – one that's helped people like Martin Clunes sustain a career in television for over 30 years – but it's also rooted in a very real, very destructive notion of masculinity: which the Oxford Dictionary defines as the 'possession of the qualities traditionally associated with men'. We're conditioned from an early age to believe that acknowledging weakness is somehow a weakness in itself, and there are plenty of bleak statistics to confirm what a huge problem this is.

Even accounting for reproductive health, in any given year men are half as likely as women to visit their GP[1], and it doesn't take a genius to work out how little sense this makes: it seems pretty unlikely that women simply get ill twice as often as men. In the UK, the rate of premature deaths (under 50 years old) is one and a half times higher[2] among men than women, primarily due to cardiovascular disease, accidents, suicide and cancer – that latter cause offering perhaps the strongest evidence of men's reluctance to seek help. For example, while affecting men and women equally, skin cancer kills twice as many men[3] because we avoid addressing the issue until it's too late.

The disparity in suicide rates is another eye-opener. In spite of depression being more common in women, British men are three times more likely to take their own lives[4].

A 2012 Samaritans report[5] concluded that the social constructs of masculinity were a major cause of this imbalance, noting that 'the way men are taught, through childhood, to be "manly" does not emphasise social and emotional skills', and that, in contrast to women, 'the "healthy" ways men cope are by using music or exercise to manage stress or worry, rather than "talking"'.

Alcoholism is also significantly more prevalent in men, linked largely to self-medicating mental illness. My paternal grandfather fought in World War Two and survived by technicality alone, the untold horrors he'd seen gouging away at his sanity until he was able to do little else but drink. Born six years after D-Day, my dad grew up like so many baby-boomers, with a father whose deep emotional repression left him unable to love, let alone talk about any of his feelings. It's a hereditary condition: men raised by men unable to communicate emotionally, the symptoms of what we now know as PTSD becoming synonymous with masculinity. It's all *wildly* fucked up when you stop to consider it.

Of course, the destruction doesn't end there. While widowed mothers deal with the fallout of our distrust for doctors, men are doing a terrific job of sabotaging any attempt at romance in the first place because of our inability to communicate. Not content with merely reliving my father's death for these words, I came up with the definitely-not-terrible idea of asking my ex-girlfriend Megan to reveal the specific problems that arose during my tenure as her shitty boyfriend.

'I think the biggest thing was that your lack of communication made it difficult to process your emotions within your own self,' she said. 'Even more than your inability to communicate it to me, you were so practised at pushing things down that you'd lost touch with the reality of your emotions. So, even when I could identify a problematic situation, you would deny it. In addition to having to work through difficult issues, I first had the insurmountable task of getting you to acknowledge they were issues in the first place.'

Communication is the key to a successful relationship, as any happily-coupled person will tell you (also, not sleeping with your colleagues; that helps, too). The worst part is, we *know* this. It's been drilled into us by every book and TV show and film that deals with these kind of issues. But still we ignore it, forging ahead under the misconception that those rules only apply to others.

So what the hell can we do about it all? It's easy to write the problem off as a lost cause, too embedded in our culture for it to ever truly change. You can't alter the personality of half the world's population overnight (and thankfully so, as there's a lot to be said for self-deprecation, cynicism and low-level passive-aggression). But you can always start trying by doing one simple thing: talking. We do it every day, so why not do it when it comes to stuff that really matters? You've had a lot of practice opening and closing your mouth to make sound come out of it, just slightly alter those sounds and it could end up doing you a lot of good.

I've got much better at talking in the last couple of years, but it's still difficult, so I started instead to write down these thoughts and share them with complete strangers; it provides a sort of detachment and allows me to open up in a way I often struggle to when speaking directly to my loved ones. Of course, that's not possible for everyone and I am indeed very lucky to have been given a platform from which to talk some asinine bollocks on occasion. Much of what you just read originally appeared in an article I wrote for VICE in October 2014, titled *A Stiff Upper Lip Is Killing British Men*[6]. Ironically, that piece ended with me calling for men to take some time and address the issue in a timely fashion because I didn't want to write a whole fucking book about it. More crucially, I figured, no one wanted to *read* a whole fucking book about it since, essentially, it all came down to acknowledging the existence of something we'd prefer to remain ignorant of. Prior to publication of the piece, I had anticipated what the response might look like, imagining the bulk of the few comments it drew being an apt denial of the issues at hand; a predictable slew of below-the-line unpleasantness, and a few laddish types telling me that I just needed to, well, man up.

I would have been content with a couple of Facebook likes, the obligatory handful of sympathy tweets from my friends and an email from my mum telling me she was proud, but in my next piece I might consider the following changes to my style and content, and did I have to swear so much? – you know, mum stuff. But no, you pricks had other ideas didn't you? You had to go and show me a more hopeful and kind side to the web, you had to break down my prejudices and crush my soul with a barrage of positivity and encouraging rhetoric. You got in touch and *thanked me* for writing it.

The piece went live on a Friday morning and I prepared to go about my day as I always did, before you lot came along and I ended up spending the rest of the daylight hours in a sort of detached state, watching in awe as it made its way around the world. Much of the afternoon involved me sitting at my laptop occasionally making odd, confused whimpering noises, punctuated with maniacal laughter and a lot of instances of me asking 'what the actual fuck is going on?' Journalists and writers I greatly admire began praising the article. Irvine Welsh called it 'fabulous': the twisted, fucked up, incredible mind that created Francis Begbie thought my whine about dead dads was good, which was hardly a reaction I'd expected.

In its first few hours of life, *A Stiff Upper Lip...* clocked up tens of thousands of shares around the world and saw praise from the kind of people writers want to be praised by. It was an awful lot of fun, if I'm being honest. After the initial shock subsided, I started to ask *why* this had happened. What about it had turned heads and ignited conversation? I briefly considered the fact that just maybe I was a brilliant writer, until I read my own clumsy words again and remembered I don't understand the most basic grammar. (I'm not kidding when I say about 90% of the time I'm totally winging it – thank fuck for editors.) So with that theory buried, it looked likely that the answer lay in a truth most people accepted long ago, but which had rarely been discussed.

While I was largely writing about a personal experience, its universality became clear. Every single person who read that piece could relate to it. In my father they saw themselves, their own fathers, their brothers, their boyfriends. For so many people to identify with a middle aged, Lycra-adorned pharmaceutical sales rep from the Midlands was astounding, but it indicated how desperate we were as a society to have this conversation. So that brings us to MAN UP.

In those initial 1,500 words I covered a few themes in a very shallow way. There's a lot more to say about these themes, and a whole world of topics to address for the first time. I don't want this book to be a judgment on any individual, because that's precisely the attitude that has caused so much upset and illness already. I want this to be a book for every man, and, particularly, 'the everyman'. Most of us, myself included, don't have a grounding in gender studies or sociology, and I don't want this to be a dry, academic tome – because otherwise you're not going to get through it. Hell, I wouldn't be able to get through it! But I will pull in experts where needed, because I am not every man and I want intelligent stats behind what I'm saying; I'll be tackling these issues head on, and on behalf of all of us.

In the interests of those idly thumbing through this introduction, trying to figure out if it's worth your time, let's just get this out of the way. Who is this book for? This book is for everyone who is in some way affected by masculinity (put simply, this book is for everyone). Our societal perception of masculinity brings harm not only to emotionally-stunted men, but to every single person who inhabits this world regardless of gender, sexuality or any other factor. *What the hell*, you say, *you can't just tell us your book's about something that obviously affects everybody in some respect and implore us all to read it.* Totally can, mate. Totally can.

But I digress. The reaction seemed very apt. This discussion on masculinity and a stiff upper lip had not really happened before, hindered, presumably, by masculinity and a stiff upper lip, which I think was largely why so many people cared. By the time I showed up to my weekend job at the Buffalo Bar in Islington that evening, I'd had to turn off all notifications on my phone. I sat in the office on a break and had a quick peek at Twitter, where I saw Irvine Welsh's comment. Excitedly, I told Michael, the manager, and he demanded I get the piece up on the computer so he could read it, which he did, and praised me for it. If you had the good fortune of meeting Michael Buffalo before developers turfed us out of that building, you might understand why that was such an exciting moment for me: with his thick Geordie accent, foul mouth and occasional tendency to refer to customers as cunts, to their faces (in his defence, only when they were really being cunts), this was a man you'd have no trouble describing as 'traditionally'* masculine – and so his approval meant a lot.

A few days later I got a text from my old housemate Cameron. I love Cam to bits, but as someone who works in finance and bases his free time largely around sport, he's embedded in what I'd call a pretty laddish culture, and he and I are very different people. In his text, he told me that he'd read the piece and loved it, and that it made him think a lot about his own inability to talk. His words are a big part of why I'm writing this. Pleasing the very liberal, social-justice types I tend to surround myself with is one thing – but getting through to Cam made me realise what a powerful thing this debate could be. More than anything, it gave me hope that maybe, gradually, we could make a difference, bit by bit.

As I write this in January 2016, I can't help but notice what a whirlwind 15 months it's been for masculinity and the conversations about men we've started to have. Last year saw the rapper Professor Green explore his father's death in the beautiful documentary *Suicide and Me*, which felt like a real breakthrough in how we approach that devastating issue. But we also watched

---

* I draw your attention to the quotes here, for reasons that should become clear as the book goes on

Reggie Yates delve into the world of 'Pick Up Artists' and show us a darker, more regressive side to men and masculinity. Men's Rights Activists – a kind of ginger group for antifeminists – have continued to harass and blame women for the woes faced by the male gender. Toxic masculinity – a phrase I will be coming back to regularly throughout this book – has driven violence, mass murder and rape just like it always has. Some of it's getting better, much of it is not. We need to address this before it's too late, for the sake of every last one of us.

If he'd learned to open up a bit more, maybe my dad wouldn't have spent his life avoiding help and would still be here. He could have spared the world yet another gratuitously self-indulgent book penned by a millennial about an emotionally distant late father, and I'd have someone to mutter at me disapprovingly every time I mentioned how my career and housing situation and life was going. Hypotheticals will get us nowhere, but until we address our inability to open up, we'll continue to die early and needlessly, and destroy the relationships we have while we're here. It may not start a revolution, but if even just a handful of people read about why we've ended up like this, how we're hurting those around us, and what we can do to make men more of a force for good in this world, then it'll be worth the fucking hours I slaved over online forums discussing when to use 'that' vs 'which', and the crushing realisation that I'll probably never remember.

What Makes a Man?

B efore I launch into the mammoth task of breaking down what I believe are the most important issues surrounding masculinity today and then try to find some sort of solutions for all of our flaws, afflictions and destructive behaviours in the hope of improving mankind for the rest of our time on Earth, I should take a moment to establish what, exactly, a man is. (There's probably some other stuff I need to think about prior to embarking on this mission as well, like 'what the fuck am I doing writing a book, this was a terrible idea, I want to get off, oh god, oh god, this is a disaster', but it's nothing a night on Yahoo Answers won't fix, I'm sure.)

In theory, this ought to be the least complicated part of the entire book. We all know what a man is, right? Great, next chapter: I am *acing* this writing thing. But while once upon a time this would have been the case, in 2016 we have a much broader understanding and acceptance of gender which doesn't conform to the binary definition we tended to use historically. You might have heard an older relative talk about how 'it used to be so much simpler, when men were men and women were women' after reading something in the paper about transgender people. Hell, you may well have thought that yourself, a lot of this is very new to many of us and it's okay to admit you're a little lost – as long as you're not going to be a dick about it. We're all here to learn (I hope) and although some readers will already be famil- iar with the terms I'm about to discuss, I'd urge these ones to stick with this chapter all the same because it might give you a bit of insight into how I'm approaching certain ideas and clear up your questions about some potentially dubious passages later on. I also like the power of forcing you to read every last one of my utterly disposable words, because I'm a bastard.

If I start this by saying we need to look at three catego- ries, all of which are interwoven but also entirely separate, I'm not going to be winning any awards for clarity. But bear with me, as I try to make sense of sex, sexuality and gender; what unites them, what separates them, and why any of this matters at all.

Sex

This might be the easiest to explain. Sex is biological, it's what we assign babies at birth based on their genitals, and in most cases this is one of two options. If a penis you see, a boy he be; if a vagina down there, then, I dunno, I quickly lost interest in this rhyme, but your baby's getting marked down as a girl on its birth certificate. Unless your parents are super-progressive, the chances are that your assigned sex at birth will be reflected in your upbringing and you will be encouraged to follow an explic- itly gendered path, based entirely on your tiny infant organs.

Less commonly, a baby may be born with a reproductive system that doesn't fit the traditional definitions of male or female sexual anatomy and may display elements of both, which is termed **intersex**. This may be apparent at birth or may not become so until later on in life, and sometimes intersex people (including infants and children) undergo surgery or hormone replacement in order to visibly conform to a binary gender.

Sexuality

A person's sexuality is who, if anyone, they are sexually attracted to (specifically, in this situation, which gender or genders). In the traditional view, **heterosexual** or **straight** people are exclusively attracted to people of the opposite gender, **homosexual** or **gay** people are exclusively attracted to people of the same gender, and **bisexual** people are attracted to both men and women. There are further labels once we step outside these binaries, such as **pansexual**, which refers to an attraction to all genders – including people who don't identify as either male or female – while some people prefer more ambiguous terms like **queer**, for example, which may simply be used as an umbrella description for anyone who's not heterosexual.

Gender

In most parts of MAN UP, this is the most important category. Gender is about personal identity, and is defined not by any physical characteristics but by an individual's mind. It's also, arguably, a social construct, a theme I'll be coming back to frequently throughout the book. A **cisgender*** person is someone whose gender matches the sex they were assigned at birth, which is the majority of people. A **transgender** person is someone whose gender does not match the sex they were assigned at birth, so someone who identifies as a woman but was born with what we traditionally consider male genitals is a transgender woman, or trans woman, or, better yet, simply a woman. Some trans people undergo sex reassignment surgery in order to change their physical body so it aligns with their gender, but this is not the case for everyone. It doesn't stop there, though, because some folks don't identify as either male or female. **Non-binary** or **genderqueer** people may identify with aspects of traditional ideas of both men and women, or neither, and often choose to be referred to by gender-neutral (they/their) or other pronouns.

Are you still with me?

Well, are you? I hope so, because there's obviously going to be a fair bit of talk about men in this book. More importantly, there's going to be a lot of talk about masculinity, particularly masculinity at its most toxic. As far as I'm concerned anyone who identifies as a man, is a man; and because masculinity is a social construct and thus rooted mostly in identity rather than

---

* The linguists among you might be interested to hear that while 'cisgender' is a relatively new term, the etymology of its component parts goes back hundreds of years. 'Cis' meaning 'on this side' was originally used when referring to places, so 'cisatlantic' would refer to the near side of the ocean while 'transatlantic' would refer to both sides of or, indeed, crossing, the ocean.

biology, masculine behaviour is exhibited by all men. Having said that, for the purposes of this book, I'm going to be looking at particular types of men much more than others, and while I will touch upon issues facing gay and trans men, as a cis, hetero-sexual ('cishet') man myself, I can't in good conscience speak for these groups because I do not have the lived experience they do. Furthermore, a lot of the behaviour I'll be exploring is quite specific to cishet guys (or at least a fair bit more prevalent within this group) – for instance, I'll be looking at how particular kinds of showy hyper-masculinity are bred by a fear that others will think we're homosexual, and, unsurprisingly, openly gay men don't tend to be quite so bothered by that.

At certain points, the focus of the book will be what I guess you might call cis- or hetero-normative; at others it'll be broader. For the sake of a clean, consistent writing style, I won't always specify if I'm referring mostly to cisgender men, and in general things should be clear from the context. Similarly, a lot of the book will cover gender in a traditional binary light, making comparisons between men and women. This is not intended to erase or ignore non-binary genders, but is something I feel is necessary for understanding particular issues because mascu-linity is in itself a result of the concept of binary genders (to the extent that it regularly manifests itself as the polar opposite of femininity).

I don't doubt that there will be people reading this who feel like these clarifications are an embarrassing sign of excessive political correctness, who think that I shouldn't need to even acknowledge such issues, and they're absolutely entitled to hold this opinion. I can't hear them, though, because that's not how books work, so I just get to keep ploughing on with the stuff that pisses them off, and that feels great. In all seriousness, this does matter to me, and if you're open-minded enough to accept that problems such as male suicide need to be addressed, then you might eventually understand why I bothered with this section at all.

If you've made it this far and have a problem with anything I've written – maybe you disagree that anyone who identifies as a man is one – there's a good chance I'll discuss it in further detail later on and you might even find it changes your mind. Essentially, what I'm saying is: just get on with it and turn to the next page. Scared? Man the fuck up. (And discover why telling people to man up is a *terrible* idea.)

The Dawn of Man

Why do men behave the way they do?

'Men, am I right?!' would be the opening line to my hypothetical, sub-Michael McIntyre, observational comedy show, because, like, *men, am I right?!* No, but seriously, what's up with men? There is no simple answer to this question, as I discovered shortly after I agreed to write this book and immediately began to regret every choice in my life that had led me to this point and wondered vaguely if my old boss at the greengrocer's stall on the market would let me come back to work.

The male mind, being human and all, and humans, being the most uniquely complex, intelligent and technologically advanced creatures ever to walk the Earth and all, is still in many ways a mystery to scientists. While medicine has given us a thorough understanding of our physical bodies and how they work, much of the human brain is completely unchartered territory. Even in more familiar areas of study like those of certain mental illnesses, which we've been able to address to some degree, it's not uncommon for psychologists to know that a particular treatment works, but to have absolutely no idea *why* it works. As far as I can see, developing treatments for the brain involves a load of scientists rummaging through the junk drawers in their homes and throwing whatever they can find at the patient until something seems to help. Marbles, solder, electrical tape, that Sports Direct mug that apparently everyone in Britain owns but without any recollection of how it came into their possession – anything they can get their hands on, until finally, when it does the trick, they mumble something about how they believe it stimulates certain synapses to produce a chemical they just made up. Basically.

So while we have some theories about behavioural tendencies, it's not something conclusive in the way 'exposure to radiation is gonna fuck you up' is. That said, we can narrow things down a bit and categorise them so it's a little less complicated. There are two main areas in which to explore influence on our gender roles: **biology** and **sociology**.

Gender as a social construct has been shaped in a big way by the historical dominance of biology, and in many ways still reflects this, despite there no longer being any real reason for it beyond that weird human desire to adhere to tradition even when it's objectively more harmful to our society than progression. In this chapter I'll be exploring both in separate sections, although there's an immense amount of crossover in each. While biology will delve much farther back, to the beginnings of human existence as we know it, sociologically I feel there's much more to be gained from focusing on very modern history (mostly the last century and a bit) for reasons that will become clear.

How biology came to define our gender roles

The evolutionary nature of the human race makes it difficult to pinpoint exactly when people became the people we know today: when we first started to display the characteristics that separated us from the primates who came before us. Anatomically modern humans evolved around 200,000 years ago, but it wasn't until 150,000 years later that it's believed we first achieved behavioural modernity – the traits that distinguished us from the previous Homo sapiens. In the context of modern masculinity, none of this is hugely important, but for the sake of definition we could quite safely say that it was around 50,000 years ago with the dawn of behavioural modernity that these male primates first became men.

While it may seem odd for me to mention this before leaping forward 49,800 years or so, this era is notable for gender being dictated by nature and not society. Up until 10,000 years ago, humans existed as hunter-gatherers and it was solely the biological differences between men and women that defined their roles. Women cared for the children and foraged, while the physically larger and stronger men were charged with the hunt. Some of the evolutionary characteristics each took on are still apparent today – such as women having more cones in their eyes, which it is believed gave them sharper vision and thus helped them gather fruits and vegetables more efficiently. Because of this, some people believe certain behaviours are also inherent within the genders as a biological condition rather than their having been socialised: aggression and violence, for example, are traits of masculinity because they may once have aided in our hunting ability. Testosterone ('the male hormone') is often blamed for the prevalence of this sort of behaviour in men, but the evidence to support this is far from conclusive, and while it's likely our physical traits (such as size) are evolutionary, there is little to suggest most behaviours aren't a result of upbringing and society. It may seem unimportant in the grand scheme of things, but this biologically-centred theory can have genuinely harmful consequences.

When people defend male aggression as an inevitable part of our nature, it's simply a way for men to avoid taking responsibility for their shitty behaviour, and allows them to inwardly justify a dangerous attitude on account of it being perceived as masculine. It writes off tens of thousands of years of human evolution, during which empires rose and fell repeatedly, intricate languages developed, our ways of life changed beyond recognition, and technology advanced to the point where practically all the information in existence was available en masse and you could communicate instantly with a person on the other side of the globe. Our minds grew to allow us infinite creative potential, we filled the world with art and music and literature, turned food from a necessity into a form of sheer pleasure, cured and inoculated ourselves against countless diseases, made passenger flight a reality, walked on the moon, sent a robot to Mars... and you punched a guy in the face because your brain momentarily confused him with a woolly mammoth?

More than anything, these arguments tend to be reserved almost exclusively for otherwise unjustifiable opinions. Take a run of the mill 'gay sex is unnatural' homophobe and consider his day: he's woken before sunrise by an alarm, puts on his polyester slippers, throws a couple of slices of Wonder Bread in the toaster, hops in his car to work, sits at his desk for eight hours, drives back home, flicks on the TV and there, being transmitted live in his living room, is a news story about gay marriage. 'It's just not natural,' he thinks, taking himself off to bed and setting his alarm for another day. This idea that homosexuality is unnatural stems mostly from the belief that sex exists solely as a means of reproduction – and thus any heterosexual activity that doesn't result in pregnancy is equally as wrong. Granted, some religious attitudes concerning people deriving any kind of pleasure from sex adhere to this, with everything from contraception to masturbation being viewed as a plague on their efforts to be fruitful and multiply, but, for the most part, in 2016 this is seen as an outdated vision. Yes, it's almost certain our sexual desire is founded in a basic instinct to ensure the future of our bloodline and it has served us almost too well – but our behaviour has evolved so far beyond this. We have sex to reproduce – sometimes – but more often than not, we have sex because it feels really good. Like most of our behaviour in the modern age, it's got nothing to do with nature, which was the point I was obviously making with the homophobic office worker: our lifestyles are so detached from those of our hunter-gatherer ancestors in virtually every way imaginable that it is absurd to claim anything is either an inherent part of our nature which we cannot alter or vice versa. Fifty thousand years have passed since humans first started exhibiting characteristics common to the uniquely intelligent creatures we are today, and it's been 10,000 years since we ceased to exist as simple hunter-gatherers, and you want to ignore literally all of civilisation's growth and say we should behave exactly as we did back then?

Much of the justification for this seems to be down to how closely our physical bodies resemble those from the past, suggesting these roles remain pertinent – otherwise men would have ceased to be bigger and stronger than women in general. The fact is, physical evolution is an incredibly slow process. Look at how we're all still born with an appendix: an organ that serves only to occasionally become inflamed and, if left untreated, to kill us. Scientists don't even know for certain what function the appendix once served, it may have been for the digestion of certain leaves but that's merely a theory. Our bodies evolve over many millennia, but our behaviour and beliefs change drastically between generations. Consider our social and political views: it's rare for a generation to be more conservative than the one directly preceding it, and by extension any before that one too. If you look at the societal change we have made in the last century, it's clear none of this would have been possible had each subsequent generation not favoured more progressive policies. That's not to say there haven't been blips of conservatism throughout, an inevitable side effect of democracy in a historically two-party system, as well as fear-mongering and scapegoating at times of economic hardship; current rhetoric surrounding immigration and the widespread dehumanisation by the media of refugees fleeing war zones can be practically indistinguishable from the anti-Semitism spouted in the 1930s and 40s as European Jews sought asylum from the Nazis in Britain. For the most part, though, we are moving forward. Indeed, it was under a Conservative prime minister that gay marriage was legalised in 2013 – twenty-five years after his party had introduced Section 28 of the Local Government Act, which banned the discussion of homosexuality in schools. Legalising gay marriage was hardly an act of political bravery, though: instead it merely reflected the views of the majority of the public and showed that even under the rule of a less traditionally progressive party we are not necessarily taking steps backwards.

I mention gay marriage not only as proof of how quickly humans can change their belief system and behaviour, but to highlight how uncommon and unfounded the idea is that such an act is 'unnatural'. This argument is thrown out there most often by people who don't want to admit that they simply find the idea of gay sex a little bit 'icky' – generally speaking, few of us would consider this a legitimate thought. Acceptance and support for gay rights today is a decidedly unradical stance, and I'm regularly amused to see outlets that were previously criticised for homophobia or misogyny such as The LAD Bible flying the rainbow flag. Everyone's cool with the gays now, they're just like us! They're normal! They're not unnatural! So why, then, do so many people still believe that gender plays such inflexible roles in work and home life?

Liberal as we may now be, and whatever evidence you may try to present to the contrary, the fact is that most of western society still favours the nuclear family headed by a man as the main financial provider, with women expected to put motherhood above all else. 'Having it all' is the phrase that's come to define the debate over whether women can be successful careerists and raise a family, and it is always women to whom it refers. Structural barriers that affect both men and women prevent most families deviating from this: in single-income households, the wage gap means that in most cases it doesn't make sense financially for a woman to be the sole earner because she is not capable of bringing in as much money as a man doing the same job. In many countries, further incentive for mothers to be the primary carer of children over fathers results from inequalities in law: statutory maternity leave tends to be much more gener- ous than paternity leave, and while efforts have been made in recent years to address this disparity, it is still harder for fathers wanting to become the primary child carer.

This has further, profound consequences on gender equal- ity. Women are routinely looked over for jobs by sexist employers who worry they will become pregnant and cost the company time and money, particularly in countries with statutory mater- nity leave laws. Anti-discrimination laws in most countries mean it's generally illegal for employers to do this, but it can be diffi- cult to prove that the employer's decision not to hire a woman was motivated by this reason. A female candidate may be the most experienced and competent candidate for a job, but the employer's fear that they may be forced to pay her for a period in which she won't contribute to the company can often lead to less suitable male candidates being hired instead, with the employer believing that the higher revenue a female candidate might gen- erate is outweighed by the cost of paying her maternity leave.

Cash rules everything around me

Unsurprisingly, this has been an issue women have been fight- ing against for a long time, but while historically this tended to be focused on income inequality and improving the employment prospects of women, in recent years more people have started to explore how this affects men in a negative way too. What I'm about to tell you may shock you to the core, so hold onto your hats: one of the biggest motivators in life is money. Money's great, you can buy and do things with it, and very few people wouldn't like more of it. As a result, men haven't traditionally been too concerned about a system from which they personally benefit, even if it's ostensibly unfair.

> 'Mike, how would you like to earn slightly less so Sandra down the hall, who does the exact same job as you and just as well if not better than you, can earn a little more?'
> 'Um. Well boss, not really. What could I possibly gain from this?'
> 'A fairer society for your children to grow up in.'
> 'But I'd earn less money?'
> 'Yes.'
> 'I'll pass.'

If you look at the super-rich, apart from a handful of the warm, cuddly, philanthropic types like Warren Buffet and Richard Branson, the income they donate to charitable causes is often smaller, percentage-wise, than what's donated by those in the poorest section of society. When most of us read about the wealth of these super-rich people, it's so enormous that we can't even fathom quite how much money that is, or how we could possibly begin to spend it. Imagine what you'd do with, say 2.5 million pounds. That'd be nice wouldn't it? And it's not totally out of the question: maybe you'll win the lottery. If you lived to 100, that'd give you £25,000 a year for every year of your life; and that includes all the ones before you started earning money. That's almost the same as the average UK wage, so as long as you kept that £2.5 million in a savings account to keep up with inflation and didn't do anything foolish, you'd never have to work a day in your life. Imagine having enough money that you never had to work! Imagine how wonderful that would be. Now imagine what you'd do with that times a thousand. That's £2.5 billion, which would be enough for you to live to 100 without working a *thousand* times over. In 2015, there were 1,826 billionaires in the world, with an average of US$3.8 billion[7] each, which at the time of writing converts to just a little bit less than your £2.5 billion. So if these 1,826 people spread their riches out to provide themselves with an average annual income, each of them would have enough money to live for 100,000 years without ever having to work. To put this in perspective: with just 10 percent of that journey elapsed, they would be as far from the present day as the era when we first began to ditch the hunter-gatherer lifestyle. Halfway through, they'd have lived as long as modern human behaviour has existed. By the time they'd blown all their cash, they'd probably be regretting this decision and questioning why they'd decided to live comfortably for 100,000 years and *Christ, it's fucking hot on Earth these days isn't it?*

That's how much money the average billionaire has. Many of these people continue to work and devote their lives to making that number grow even further, because that's what money does: it distorts your perspective. For many humans, no matter how money much they have, they will always want more. Regardless of our situation, we are rarely satisfied and know it can always be better. It's one of the things that makes humans so unique, and although it can seem baffling on a scale such as this, it's probably the reason we've become so technologically advanced: there is always something else that can improve our lives.

So when Mike's boss asks him if he wants to earn a little less so Sandra down the hall can earn a little more, regardless of whether he knows it's the fair thing to do, he won't personally sacrifice the thing that motivates him. It's human nature that those with the most privilege, even when they know this is the case and recognise how unfair it is, are reluctant to give it up. The comedian Louis CK explained this in the context of race better than perhaps anyone could:

> I love being white. Seriously, I really do. If you're not white, you're missing out: 'cause this shit is thoroughly good. Let me clear this up by the way: I'm not saying white people are better. I'm saying that *being* white is clearly better. Who could even argue? If it was an option I would re-up every year! "Oh yeah, I'll take white again. Absolutely." Here's how great it is to be white: if I would have a time machine I could go to any time and it would be awesome when I get there! That is exclusively a white privilege! Black people can't fuck with time machines!

Men have always benefited from their gender when it comes to work, and continue to do so, even though for many of us it's in no way intentional or malicious. It is crucial that we recognise this: if you believe women deserve equal chances, you must at least acknowledge the problem exists. If you don't believe women deserve equal chances then you probably shouldn't be reading this book, but even then, there is an incentive to make yourself aware of these issues, because it can benefit you as a man too.

How we designed our way out of our biological destinies

As gender roles have shifted over the past 60 or 70 years more women have gone into work and have gradually started to achieve positions of seniority previously held exclusively by men (197 of those 2015 billionaires were women, the highest number ever). Financially, men are still significantly more powerful, but more and more frequently we are seeing what once would have been unthinkable: households and partnerships in which women are the main earner. At the same time, this has presented men an opportunity rarely offered in the past: to be the primary carer of their children.

This is one of the key examples of how biology is now a redundant factor in gender roles. While it is true that their physical size and strength gave early men an edge as hunters, women, given the chance, would also have been capable of the muscle gain required to take on their prey, despite being naturally smaller. Men, by contrast, would have been unable to fulfil the role of child carer because they lack the ability to produce milk – a fact I sometimes lament when I gaze in the mirror at my inexplicable set of functionless nipples. And so it was writ, for most of history, that gender roles would be dictated not by what women *could do* but by what men *could not*. It is the cruellest of ironies, and still today women suffer for what some might suggest is in fact their biological superiority. However, this need not be the case.

Wet nurses, used by mothers unable or unwilling to feed their baby, have an ancient history: but thanks to the advent of breast pumps and formula milk, infants are no longer reliant on direct access to mammary glands. Though relatively simple concepts, these inventions are responsible for one of the most revolutionary blows to gender roles in history, allowing men to become the primary child carer and giving women the opportunity to return to work almost immediately. They also paved the way, logistically speaking, for adoptions by same-sex couples (although it would be many decades before social and legal acceptance caught up). After hundreds of thousands of years of gender roles enforced by biology, the only physical barrier preventing a father raising his child had been destroyed. We invented our way out of a biologically enforced structure, do you realise how amazing that is? Up yours, mother nature, you're not our real mum anyway!

Socially, we've still a long way to go, but attitudes can be changed much quicker than bodies. It's only in the past two or three decades that this has taken visible effect, but it's clear that every year more men are learning to embrace fatherhood in a massive way and for some reason it seems that every last one of them is being given a broadsheet column to discuss this. (Seriously, is this all it takes? Because I will absolutely father a child if it means I have a lucrative regular writing gig.) It also seems to be affecting wider attitudes on fatherhood, with even dads who work full time starting to focus more attention on bonding with their offspring. I will address the wider social implications of this in more detail later in the book, but it goes without saying that this is already having a positive effect on our perceptions of masculinity, and will play a crucial part in how gender roles are shaped in a future that's better for us all. Or, at least, it could. We may have knocked down the physical wall, but unless we address the sociological issues, the reality is that few men will be given such an opportunity, and that's a tragedy.

The growing cost of staying alive

Not that long ago, it was possible to raise a family quite comfortably on just the father's salary (and it was, almost universally, the father who worked). In 2015, the average cost of raising a child to the age of 21 was £229,251[8], or just under £11,000 a year. Based on a 10% deposit on a payment of £235,000[9] (which would buy you somewhere to live with two beds in Manchester), a family's mortgage would cost £15,600 annually. Before you even add basic living costs such as food (which is, you know, quite important), the mortgage plus the cost of a child exceeds the average salary of £26,000: meaning it would require a wage much higher than the average if only one parent was working. Most people don't earn a wage much higher than the average, unfortunately, because that's sort of the idea of averages, so in general, it's simply not feasible for one parent to stay at home with their child until school age.

Maternity pay takes care of some of this, ensuring that working mothers are not forced to return to employment immediately after labour. In the UK, mothers are paid 90% of their normal wage for the first six weeks, and then receive £139.58 (or 90%, whichever is lower) for the next 33 weeks. Fathers are given paid paternity leave for just two weeks. It wasn't until the Second World War that the concept of women in the workplace took off, ergo: it wasn't until the forties when paid leave for parents was actually a necessity. And that was just one period out of many in the last couple of hundred years that's so important to look at in terms of how we see masculinity today.

We are not amused

I know, I know, there's no proof Queen Victoria ever said those words, but frankly I don't think it matters because, either way, they conveniently sum up the spirit of the period to which she gave her name. Britain in the 19th century is uniquely fascinating to many of us today. It was pretty miserable for most of society, as was always the case historically, but it was also a time of great wealth for the country itself. It spawned some of (arguably) the most beautiful buildings and came to define much of what we now consider intrinsic values of Britishness. Even ideals such as our desire for a white Christmas can be linked back almost entirely to the writing of Charles Dickens, whose work reflected the period of what is now considered to have been a mini ice age. It was also the beginning of a culture of etiquette and properness.

Ask a sample of foreigners what they believe to be the key defining characteristic of the average Briton, and I guarantee more often than not their answer will be 'politeness'. We've built a reputation as a sometimes infuriatingly polite society, of which George Mikes – a Hungarian-born writer transplanted to London in his twenties – famously wrote in *How to Be an Alien*: 'An Englishman, even if he is alone, forms an orderly queue of one.' This focus on etiquette, which presumably began as a side-effect of the emergent Victorian middle class, was responsible for forming the very conservative attitudes we've come to be known for today, many of which, by extension, have mutated into qualities we now perceive (often incorrectly) as being masculine: such as emotional repression. Such was the influence of the Victorian era on what's now synonymous with 'British values', it's easy to assume we've always been prudes, emotionally and sexually repressed, offended by the slightest suggestion of impropriety – but go back a couple of hundred years before the Victorians and you'll find British literature was *filthy*. And I don't mean 'ooh er, look at her flashing her ankles' filth, but legitimate filth that wouldn't make it past the television censors even today. Take this excerpt from John Wilmot, the Earl of Rochester's *A Ramble In St James's Park* written in 1672:

> Had she picked out, to rub her arse on,
> Some stiff-pricked clown or well-hung parson,
> Each job of whose spermatic sluice
> Had filled her cunt with wholesome juice,

Wilmot died eight years later of venereal disease, because *of course he did*. If that was what passed for poetry in the 17th century (poetry, for god's sake!) I dread to think what porn was like back then. Go even further back to the time of Chaucer; sex and profanity abound. My point is, we weren't always the boring, sexless prudes suggested by the phrase 'British values'; not that long ago we were pretty loud and open about our sexuality, but the Victorians helped put an end to that. If we continue down the 'what poetry teaches us about our history' road, Rudyard Kipling's 'If—', one of the most famous poems of all time, is basically an ode to the stiff upper lip. Published in 1895, it tells the reader that if he can follow a set of rules (for example: 'never breathe a word about your loss'), he'll 'be a Man, my son.' Suffice to say, by the time the 20th century rolled around, Brits – especially men – were well on their way to being the emotionally troubled messes we know them as today.

Turns out a few things change after two world wars...

As globalisation in the late 19th and early 20th century set in, the world transformed like it never had before. In fact, although there had already been movement and trading across the continents for hundreds of year by this point, it was the first time the world really began to function as something more than a collection of individual states. Given the nature of humans, it's no surprise that this period saw the first two World Wars take place barely two decades apart, and while globalisation itself wasn't the catalyst for these conflicts, the changing nature of how we did business and the increasing co-dependency between international allies made it almost inevitable that war was now going to be fought on a much larger scale. This, of course, meant that Britain had access to more manpower; the flip side of this was that so did our enemies.

Having historically avoided conscription, when war broke out in 1914, the secretary of state for war, Lord Kitchener, tried to find ways of encouraging as many men as possible to sign up. On the assumption that men would be more willing to serve their country if they could do so alongside their friends and family, the so-called Pals Battalions were set up. These comprised men who enlisted together in local recruitment drives, and they proved enormously successful, as journalist and historian Bruce Robinson notes[10]:

> Lord Derby was the first to test the idea when he announced in late August that he would try to raise a battalion in Liverpool, comprised solely of local men. Within days, Liverpool had enlisted enough men to form four battalions.
>
> Liverpool's success prompted other towns and cities to follow suit. This was the great secret behind the Pals: civic pride and community spirit prompted cities to compete with each other and attract the greatest possible number of new recruits.

Although the idea succeeded in its goal to increase manpower, it decimated the male populations of entire streets and towns across the country. As if the lives claimed by the enemy weren't devastating enough, 306 British soldiers were executed in the war for crimes that wouldn't have carried the death penalty in civilian life. For many, their conviction was for cowardice. Today, with a better understanding of mental health, it's generally accepted that most of these men were afflicted by post-traumatic stress disorder and their supposed crimes were not the result of conscious decisions. As recently as 1993, the then-Prime Minister John Major refused to pardon the men, maintaining that they were tried fairly and that doing so would be an insult to those who died honourably on the battlefields. This policy was eventually reversed by Blair-era defence secretary Des Browne, but only in 2006.

Never before had so many men fought for their country. The men who survived did so after having been warped by the strict rules of military culture. The executions for cowardice were as much a warning as a punishment: if you succumb to even a moment of weakness, you too will meet your end by firing squad at dawn. This was drilled into the recruits with such severity that the effects were often irreversible, and on their return they didn't stand a chance of reintegrating into healthy society. Though hailed as heroes, they were betrayed by their government and mostly left to suffer in silence with their physical and mental wounds.

Once upon a time war was something British men chose to participate in, but with the introduction of conscription in WW1 and a return to it when war broke out again in 1939, the first half of the 20th century marked a notable turning point in how the country built its forces. Conscription obviously applied only to men, because only men were eligible to serve in the armed forces at this time, but it is worth noting all the same.

The association between masculinity and the military may have been cemented centuries before WW1, but conscription revolutionised how society saw men by removing their free will and forcing them to conform. In other words, it made their masculinity compulsory.

By taking away a man's ability to choose whether or not he went to war, there was now a new, state-sanctioned require-ment for masculinity. Conscientious objectors who refused to fight risked imprisonment, but perhaps more significantly they faced severe social ostracism, and even today they continue to be considered cowardly by some. On an episode of Question Time in 2009, Nick Griffin (the-then leader of the far right British National Party) responded to accusations by Jack Straw (who, at the time, was Justice Secretary) that he was a Nazi supporter by pointing out that while his father had served in the RAF during WW2, Straw's was locked up 'for refusing to fight Adolf Hitler'[11]. Undeniably a cheap shot, the incident did however highlight the enduring stigma surrounding conscientious objectors. There's no doubt that vast numbers of the men who fought did so reluctantly, but there was a widespread acknowledgement that serving your country was simply your duty as a man, some-thing you just had to accept and get on with. Conscription was removed for the last time in 1960, by which point it had been a reality for two generations of British men, and though the law may have changed, the attitudes it created in society were firmly in place and ready to be passed on to the kids of the future.

I'll keep this brief, since I've already touched upon the emotional toll of war and will return to the military in more depth later, but it's important: it wasn't just the service itself that was compulsory – everything that came afterwards was also mandated. You were expected to get on with life as normal, and when any problems arose – particularly those concerning mental health – you had to just suck it up like everyone else. Because it was compulsory, because you were one of so many who'd gone through the exact same shit as you, because you weren't special or unique, there was a pressure to shake it off like all the others seemed to, to act like all the other men. And so, by extension, what became the norm among men in society grew to be seen as a masculine trait. Masculinity, at its core, is simply a reflection of how the majority of men act, and when some event changes a large percentage of the male population, what we consider to be masculine changes with it.

...but it isn't all bad for everybody

It wasn't just men who found their gender roles changing during this time. The Second World War was instrumental in what was arguably the biggest breakthrough for women's rights: their widespread introduction to the workplace*. With a good portion of its working-age men conscripted to the forces, the UK turned to its women to fill the gaps the men had left, employing them in roles essential to the war effort and the continued running of the country.

The war brought with it vast change, and when it was all over in 1945, Britons were hungry for a new, fairer society. In spite of Winston Churchill being much celebrated for leading the country to victory, a general election less than two months after VE Day saw his Conservative Party lose by a landslide to Clement Attlee's Labour. After the First World War, there was

---

* Some might argue that gaining the right to vote in 1928 was more significant, but as far as I'm concerned this had much less impact on the everyday lives of most women than the ability to work, which allowed them to liberate themselves from their reliance on men to survive.

widespread resentment over government promises that had failed to materialise, such as 'homes fit for heroes'. Poorer soldiers were unhappy with having to return to a society with such tangible class divisions, after they had served as bravely as anyone. This was still fresh in the memory of a lot of people in 1945, so it was clear that this time things had to be different. It led to the establishment of the welfare state and the NHS, which continues to be a source of great national pride, but on the home front, it seemed that having proved themselves more than up to the task in the world of work, women couldn't just be expected to revert to their old roles as housewives. Gradually, they began to be a more familiar sight in workplaces, and while they were a long way off real equality (and this is still the case) the path was laid.

With women allowed to work, the number of eligible labourers in the country was essentially doubled and although they weren't yet considered as useful as men, any kind of market saturation inevitably leads to devaluation. Today, in order to support a family you generally need the incomes of two adults; half a century ago you could usually survive on one – it changed the way we work, and it changed the way we saw gender. For women, it was liberating: no longer were they bound by the men in their life in order to feed and house themselves. For men, it was a bit more complex. Traditional gender roles in society had provided men and women with a fairly consistent set of rules by which to abide, and men often took great pride in fulfilling what was expected of them: going to work and singlehandedly providing for their families gave them a sense of purpose, and in doing what only men were supposed to do, they affirmed their masculinity. As the number of women at work rose, and men watched their wives and partners get jobs, they began to lose that sense of purpose and, with it, felt their masculinity was under threat.

We can trace a lot of the more toxic aspects of modern masculinity back to this. For all the negatives associated with those traditions, they did provide men with some sort of healthy reinforcement of their masculinity. With that gone, men still needed to feel like men, and unfortunately this now had to find its origin in their behaviour and attitude. Toxic masculinity in its most basic form is overcompensation bred of insecurity: an exaggerated display of behaviours and actions perceived as being masculine. Going to work was no longer a masculine enough pursuit, so men felt the need to prove their masculinity in any other ways they could. Before you go blaming the women though, may I remind you that by this time, formula milk was easy to obtain. For a child to be raised by one of its parents in its early years of life can be wonderful for both child and parent, but there's no reason why that parent can't be the father. In the post-war period, men had all the means necessary for them to be the primary child-carer, and as a society we could so easily have decided that, now that women were working, men could stay at home and raise the family. We could have built a country where both men and women went to work, and men and women stayed at home, and partners decided between themselves which they'd prefer, and the child would be raised by a parent but it didn't matter which parent it was, as long as the child was loved. But we didn't. Women went and worked just as they'd long known they could, and proved they could do whatever men could do, and began to feel empowered and strong and independent. Men, by contrast, didn't show that they could do what women historically had done, and so, it could be argued, the problems which arose from this change were of men's own making.

A quick erosion of the British working class

The latter half of the 20th century delivered significant blows to the working class on both sides of the Atlantic. (For the best representation of this Stateside, watch season two of *The Wire* if you haven't already, but also, why haven't you watched *The Wire* already?) As globalisation continued to change the way we did business and a particularly aggressive form of capitalism was adopted by the likes of Margaret Thatcher and Ronald Reagan, profit by any means was prioritised – and if that meant it was cheaper to import goods from abroad than to manufacture them at home, then so be it. British industry, once among the strongest in the world, crumbled in favour of a service-based economy. The most notorious victim of this change was the mining industry, which was decimated by closures, forcing thousands of men out of work. Some towns were centred so closely around mining that the majority of their inhabitants became unemployed, and with little in the way of job opportunities locally, poverty was rife. For a lot of the men, mining had been in the family for generations and a lack of formal education or available training meant that long-term unemployment was unavoidable. The scars left by this societal change remain today, and in some of the hardest hit areas there is now a generation of adults who have never worked. Poverty and mass unemployment bring with them a whole host of other social problems: increased crime, higher rates of alcohol and drug abuse, more violence. Hopelessness and boredom combine with destructive consequences, but fractured masculinity is surely a factor too. Crime, substance abuse and violence affect everyone, but all of these issues tend to be perpetrated by a sample mostly made up of men.

If physical labour was especially male-dominated, no job carried as much weight of raw masculinity as mining. Effectively, the loss of that industry emasculated (for want of a better word) millions of working class British men, and I would argue that a good portion of the social issues that subsequently arose can be attributed to a desperate attempt by men to claw back some sense of their masculinity. Violence is inherently male: fighting other men is a public demonstration of masculinity, while domestic violence can be a show of dominance against a partner; alcohol significantly increases the risk of violent behaviour, and since drinking is a particularly male coping mechanism, the two go hand in hand. A big part of the appeal of petty crime, such as vandalism, is its associated risk, and as I'll explore further in another chapter, risky behaviour, too, is itself a trait of toxic masculinity.

The reason we are seeing toxic masculinity manifest itself in these deprived communities in the 20th century in a way that didn't previously exist (at least not to such extremes) is that there are no longer the healthy means of affirmation which kept men satisfied and secure in the past. Men need to feel secure in their masculinity, and to feel that their gender is validated somehow. If there are no societal supports for this, they are going to go looking for that validation in unsocial activities such as violence or petty crime.

The 80s, or, Oh God! What were they thinking, why the mullets? Why?

As someone who grew up in the Bush-Blair years, the 'Special Relationship' doesn't exactly have positive connotations for me, but I'd take it any day over Reagan and Thatcher. The 1980s was a whirlwind time, defined by soaring financial inequality, overindulgence and basically every aspect of capitalism that would leave an otherwise moderate liberal clamouring for Marxism. There was less manufacturing work than ever on offer, as the service-based economy took root, and this was arguably the biggest overhaul in the nature of employment in the UK since the war. Men could no longer reinforce their masculinity through physical labour, because such a thing was increasingly disappearing from the landscape, to be replaced by sedentary, corporate desk jobs – for which historically-useful biological traits such as size and strength had given men no edge over women in terms of employability. This was paralleled by the consumerism that marked the decade as a whole: luxury brands and big-name fashion labels targeted every man who had the slightest bit of disposable income with more intensity and volume than previously. For millennia, work had given men purpose and pride in their gender, but this all changed in the latter part of the 20th century. Work itself could no longer pro-vide a sense of masculinity, so now we looked to the money.

I'll return to this in the later chapter The Ideal Man, but for the sake of keeping this chapter relatively concise will move on for now.

The 90s, or, Oh God! What were they thinking, why the bucket hats? Why?

The 1990s brought with it the emergence of a new type of man: the 'lad'. As Tim Adams, a writer for *The Observer* put it[12]:

> You could say that laddism was also a very British response to the American-led backlash against feminism, championed by Robert Bly and others. In 1992, following on from the success of Bly's Iron John, a series of books appeared on the bestseller lists in the States called things like *Fire in the Belly: On Being a Man* and *King Warrior Magician Lover: Rediscovering the Archetypes of the Mature Masculine.* Bly intended his movement to be a model for how men, diminished in his view by the women's movement, could find a way to regain their self-esteem. To British eyes, this apparently looked like an excuse for one long stag party, an endless skool disco, and a host of magazines devoted to the coarse glamour of being a bloke.

It's easy to laugh off the concept of the lad or dismiss it as a relatively minor fad in the grand scheme of things, but it dominated British culture at this time – and to an extent, still does today. Britpop was the biggest homegrown musical movement the country had seen since the glory days of The Beatles and

The Rolling Stones, and while the likes of Pulp and Suede, led by their androgynous frontmen, achieved great success, the two bands with which the genre became truly synonymous were Blur and Oasis, who in August 1995 famously battled it out for the top spot in the singles charts. The rock star antics of both groups were popular tabloid fodder for years, and though the two rivals obviously had their differences, both behaved in a way that was ostensibly laddish.

The lad was spawned from a backlash to the metrosexual, 'new man' that appeared in the 80s, and was the antidote to a very middle class trend – but lad culture's own relationship with class is a little disjointed and contradictory in itself. Lads drew from what they believed were working class values, yet tended to be from middle-class backgrounds themselves; it was a movement built around appropriating and romanticising a culture to which they didn't belong. As I'm sure anyone who's been to a British university in the last decade will attest, some of the most vociferous lads are rich, privately-schooled rugby boys, often studying for high-flying degrees such as medicine or finance. Lad culture is not exclusive to this group, though, it's just as prevalent among less wealthy, non-university educated men, and those whose families would have once been considered working class. Indeed, the last clause of the previous sentence is rather revealing: *would have once been considered working class*. Because this is no longer the case: the working class itself has all but disappeared. Today, these people are members of a broader middle class, the only differences within that group being that some are much richer than others. Lad culture tries to emulate the lost working class because of its association with masculinity, but it does so in the misinformed belief that it had been a man's social standing that gave him validation, when in actual fact it was the manual work itself. The clothes, the drinking culture, the distinct push away from more 'refined' values that define the lad – all could be said to back this up, albeit in slightly offensive terms.

What I will refer to as 'toxic masculinity' is behaviour that is intended to represent an ideal of masculinity, executed by someone with a warped understanding of the subject. It is superficial, and although usually based on a historical concept of masculinity, it is removed from any of the original context that made it positive or desirable. Lad culture – in its attempts to derive a sense of manhood from an emulation of the working class while omitting the single most crucial detail of this social group (ie the work it did) is toxic masculinity incarnate. It doesn't matter if lads as individuals are progressive, if they're feminists or supportive of gay rights (as is the case more and more); the lad is a subculture built on a concept that defines toxic masculinity, and as long as lads exist, we're going to have a problem with men.

Love the sinner, hate the sin

If you don't believe me, or if that sounds like a massive over-exaggeration, ask yourself what some of the major characteristics of lad culture are. Your answers may differ from mine, but off the top of my head and based on my personal experience, some words that come to mind when I think of lads are: loud, banter, alcohol, sex, sexism, Kasabian, competition, risk, sport,

pranks, showing-off, Kasabian, gym, Kasabian. What the fuck is
the appeal of Kasabian? I hate Kasabian.

Obviously this is an entirely subjective list, and if I'd planned
ahead and actually polled people it would have been a bit more
scientific, but I think most of it would hold up under scrutiny – if
you take exception to any of those words I guess you can always
try tweeting at me for a proper argument. What makes lad culture such an important area to study is that almost every aspect
of it reflects a modern perception of masculinity, and often this
is executed in its most toxic form.

One thing you hear a lot of self-professed lads say is that
everything they do is 'just for a laugh'. They do stuff purely for
a cheap thrill, because they can. If it's at the expense of other
people it's shrugged off as 'harmless banter', and people who
challenge this are condemned as humourless prudes. It goes
deeper than that though. A group of men – loud, assertive,
unapologetic – know they can get away with a lot if they take
the piss out of someone 'for banter', as they're unlikely to be
physically challenged because of their size and number. When
men mock women, it's 'harmless banter'. And yet, women have
been assaulted, even murdered, by men upset by as little as
having their advances turned down. For women, there is no such
thing as harmless banter. Lad culture is male privilege personified. The list of things that only men can do is rapidly shrinking,
the gap is closing and soon there will be nothing left of what
has traditionally elevated us over women. Lad culture is a last
gasp, an attempt to claw back any power and dominance we can,
because we wrongly believe that these forms of behaviour are
sources from which our masculinity can be derived.

The future, or, Oh God! What's wrong with us, why with the bucket hats again? How?

Is masculinity in crisis? I don't know. Maybe. Some people say it is. Some people don't. Some other people say it is but in a totally different way to how the first people say it is, which is confusing, I know. Personally, I think 'masculinity in crisis' is too vague and ambiguous a phrase to be in any way helpful to you, or me, or really anyone who gives a shit about men. Is the need to assert our masculinity in the modern world harming us? Absolutely. Are ignorant, outdated perceptions of masculinity a problem? Yes. Most importantly, can we realistically start to address these issues in a way that will benefit every one of us, regardless of gender? I believe we can.

It won't be easy. We're up against people who don't want to see progress. We face opposition from groups who claim they support much of what we do, but only when it serves to further their hateful, divisive agendas – Men's Rights Activists (MRAs), for example, will purport to be interested in reducing the male suicide rate or fighting for abused men to have better access to shelters or counselling, yet they spend most of their time and energy coordinating online attacks against prominent feminists whom they believe are to blame for the ills men face, rather than taking affirmative action to actually address these problems. These people often say that the solution to our current 'crisis of masculinity' lies in regression, and believe that only by reverting to traditional gender roles can men be saved. Unfortunately for them, we're too far gone now and there's no chance of that ever happening. Our salvation lies elsewhere.

And so I conclude this brief history of how, over the course of

50,000 years, man came to be, with a nod to the future. Because though I am sure I've missed out a handful of details – the odd little thing here or there which shaped male behaviour in the time between me writing this chapter and the beginning of humanity as we know it – our history is of only so much use, and now we must focus on what's to come.

If masculinity is indeed in crisis, it can only be fixed by moving forwards – and I hope in the next few chapters, we can start to learn how.

Boys Don't Cry: Childhood, Social Conditioning and Mental Health in Gender

Be honest: if you saw a newborn baby clothed in pink, what sex would you assume that child was? I'm guessing your answer here is 'female', because of course it is. It doesn't make you a bad person for making that assumption, no matter how educated or progressive you consider yourself to be, because you *know* that in the vast majority of cases this is true. In the early weeks of our lives, we're all pretty much indistinguishable, and I suppose that by dressing babies in traditionally gendered colours parents feel they're giving their offspring some sort of identity beyond 'weird, hairless, noisy, miniature human'. Obviously, at this stage of development, kids have absolutely no awareness about the implications of colour and so, while it may simplify things for the parents, it doesn't seem like something that'll cause any harm to the baby's future well-being. What I mean by this is that even parents who know they will openly encourage their child to explore their sexual identity as they grow up may be inclined to dress their newborn in gender-appropriate colours, knowing that doing so will have no direct impact on the baby because it won't remember anything about this. The idea that pink = girl and blue = boy is so deeply embedded in our culture that it's almost impossible to dissociate oneself from this by the time you're old enough to begin making decisions for yourself – and while we continue to dress babies according to sex, these ideas aren't going anywhere.

It might seem like there's an easy solution to this, but as anyone who's lived a few years on this planet should know by now, nothing's ever that simple. I recently met my partner's pregnant cousin and her husband for the first time, who told me how hard it was to find gender-neutral baby clothes and accessories. I hadn't even considered until then how dependent a lot of young families are on handouts and gifts from those around them, and while they may personally be seeking out an alternative, the people around them – particularly those of older generations – may not be quite so in-tune to these issues. I suspect their family will be fully supportive of how they raise their child, but other parents are not nearly so fortunate and this is what we're up against: social change being prevented not by a lack of willingness, but by one's financial situation.

We're all sheep

As humans, so much of our behaviour and attitude is dictated by what everyone else is doing. Fashion isn't just confined to clothes: it's in our nature to conform and fit in, and if social perceptions change, we tend to try our best to match these because few people really want to be an outsider. This doesn't happen organically though, it slowly works its way into the mainstream after a lot of effort from small groups who may be painted as 'radical' at the beginning. Take gay rights, for example, something the majority of Brits support today. We didn't just decide suddenly that the gays had had a bit of a rough time and deserved the same treatment as heterosexual people: it took decades of fighting by an oppressed minority, with gradually more and more people joining the cause until it reached something of a tipping point and could no longer be ignored. Support for a cause that not too long ago could have seen you beaten up, imprisoned or even killed is now a vote winner for political parties who were once vehemently opposed to it.

I'm certainly not equating choosing baby clothes with civil rights, but it does help to illustrate how social movements spread through the masses. If a handful of 'radical' parents start dressing their babies in gender-neutral clothes, their peers will be much more inclined to follow suit, particularly if it opens up a dialogue about why they're making this choice. As this goes on, the idea spreads to a more 'mainstream' audience, and then things can change very quickly. If there's a clear demand for gender-neutral clothes, manufacturers and retailers will jump in to fill it, making it easier for everyone to access these products because there's money to be made. And after that, things can really get interesting.

The way our brains work when we're children is *fascinating*. The amount of information we are able to consume and process is phenomenal: a scholar may spend their entire life honing their knowledge of any given subject and reach the top of their field, but what they learn in decades is still nothing compared to their first few years on Earth. The ability to talk, to read and write, to understand numbers, to build and maintain relationships with other people – all of these things occur in a shorter time than it takes to gain a doctorate. It doesn't matter how much you study as an adult, it won't come close to the sheer volume and necessity of the knowledge you accrue at the very beginning. There's a good chance you're aware of how much harder it is to learn something new as you get older – I remember more of the French I learned for three years aged 11–14 than the Spanish I learned for the five years after that, even though I spent at least twice as many hours each week on the latter.

There is a downside, though: not everything we're taught as children is to our benefit, and the attitudes we pick up from the adults around us become so deeply rooted in our minds that we often struggle to shake them off as we grow up. Part of the reason I'm writing this book is because I was amazed at my own inability to change my behaviour for so long, in spite of the fact I knew it was harming me, which is why I believe it's so important to look at how our children are raised.

Our double standards when it comes to gender norms

There are very, very few situations in which gender inequality works against men rather than women: so few that I would imagine most of them are covered at some point in this book. One particular example rears its head at an important stage of development though, and, as a consequence, can do a lot of damage.

As children become more aware of the world around them, boys and girls tend to start pursuing different interests and hobbies – sometimes this happens organically, but often it's enforced by parents. The fundamental activities may be the same, but they take on a gendered angle (e.g. Barbie vs Action Man), and kids who don't conform to societal expectations are often steered away from their choices or ridiculed, even by their parents. However, there is arguably more pressure put on boys to play the 'right' way, and girls tend to be given more leeway. These girls are often referred to as being 'tomboys', and while there is plenty to criticise about this term, it's generally used in an endearing way. There's no equivalent word for boys who embrace their feminine side – not one that's used in a positive context, at least – and I don't think there's much doubt about why this is.

It remains an abomination that toy toolsets are marketed only to boys, but as attitudes towards women (especially as workers) continue to change and girls are exposed to positive role models, they stand a better chance at ignoring the labels imposed upon them. The advancement of women's rights has opened them up to what was once strictly the domain of men, but there has been no equivalent movement by men towards traditionally feminine territories; our ideals have changed little by comparison. Imagine a little girl saying she wanted to be an astronaut or a scientist or, hell, even a lorry driver, and her parents telling her: 'You can't do that, you're a woman.' Now imagine a little boy, in tears for whatever reason, being told by his parents: 'Boys don't cry.' Fifty years ago, neither of these situations would have raised an eyebrow. Today, the first would seem – to most people, I'd hope – shocking, not least because it's quite clearly not true. The second one, or some variation on that theme, I've witnessed happening in public places on multiple occasions in the last couple of years, which brings me to crux of this chapter.

Crying as catharsis

Right now, the most significant issue surrounding men and masculinity, and the one that needs to be addressed most urgently, is emotional repression. I don't think that when parents tell a boy he shouldn't cry it's necessarily a malicious thing, and their reasons may well be understandable: if he's throwing a tantrum because you wouldn't buy him a toy, I imagine it's probably quite tempting to do anything if it shuts him the fuck up. Since a lot of kids want to be treated like they're grownups, telling him that an older boy wouldn't do that 'because boys don't cry' might be an effective method, but in the heat of the moment it's likely you're not going to be considering the wider consequences of saying this, or following up on it with an explanation about when it is okay to cry. He might take it at face value and be fine, but if repeated over time there's a chance it will completely warp his idea of healthy emotions. Crying is an instinctual reaction to being overwhelmed by emotion, and I'm sure even the most hardened of men know the cathartic release it brings. We can train ourselves to avoid this, but we must also question why it exists in the first place.

Crying itself isn't really the issue, so you can relax if you were worried I was about to call for mass manly cry-athons.

The thing that matters is what crying actually does: it provides an emotional release and a means of venting. There are plenty of healthy ways to achieve this: including, most notably, talking things through with a friend, partner or therapist (at a push, yelling into a pillow can do the trick too). What you absolutely shouldn't do after overcoming the urge to cry is let yourself think: '(*Welp!*)...Managed to avoid tears, problem solved' and bottle everything up until it all gets too much. The problem with 'boys don't cry' is that it's rarely followed by a disclaimer about other emotional outlets. When you tell a child to override an instinct that appears right after his first breath, you're essentially saying that all forms of emotional expression should be avoided if he wishes to appear masculine. And it's all too likely that, if he learns that at a young age, it'll be with him forever.

Plenty of men reach adulthood and realise the absurdity of this, but it's so widespread that by this point the damage is already done: if the majority of your friends are also male, the chances are they grew up with similar attitudes and, regardless of what they currently believe, they simply don't know how to address it properly. It's one thing to identify that you need to talk about problems you're having, but being able to broach the subject for the first time is something else entirely. I mentioned earlier how much easier it is to learn new skills when you're a child, and this is no exception: being able to communicate about your emotions is vital, but so complex that learning this as an adult is a daunting task. Girls, for the most part, talk openly to each other from childhood, and as a result women tend to be much more emotionally mature. The same Samaritans report I referred to in the introduction noted that: 'Women maintain close same-sex relationships across their lives, but men's peer relationships drop away after the age of 30. Women are much more open to talking about emotions than men of all ages and social classes.' Because of this, when men do open up, it's often to their partners – and only their partners – something that can put a strain on their relationship.

When I was with my first real girlfriend, I managed to get to a stage where I was comfortable talking to her about my mental health after a lot of encouragement on her part. However, we were having a lot of problems as a couple by this point, not all of which I felt able to share with her. It was a constant cause of concern and annoyance for her that I didn't discuss our relationship with my friends in the way she did with hers – and what's worse, the fact she did this made me feel quite uneasy. Inevitably it all fell apart, but her patience and tolerance while we were together meant that I was able to address some of my major flaws and grow on an emotional level; however, I was lucky, and we can't rely on every man having a partner who can do this, because if nothing else, it's massively unfair on women.

The male suicide epidemic

Mental illness is a complex issue, and it's crucial that we talk about it carefully and make sure not to draw oversimplified links when looking at possible causes. There's a lot to be said about how being a man affects your mental health, but it's worth remembering before I go any further that these factors are just a small part of a far grander picture. In England and Wales, suicide is now the leading cause of death in men aged 20–49, and in

2013, 78% of suicides in the UK[13] were by men. Let that sink in for a second. Men are over *three times* more likely to take their own lives than women, a disparity that's disturbing on its own. But it gets even more troubling when we look at wider statistics and see that women are actually 40% more likely[14] to develop mental illnesses. At a glance this seems to suggest men are less able to cope with illnesses such as depression or anxiety; however, there are number of things we have to take into consideration. The hard data used to compile such statistics can only reflect what is *reported*, i.e. diagnoses. Men are half as likely as women to visit their GP in any given year, so we can assume that they are also more likely to be afflicted by undiagnosed illnesses. Some studies do try to factor in these sociological and cultural differences, but regardless of how educated these estimates may be, at the end of the day it's essentially just guesswork. Furthermore, there is evidence to suggest the disparity is greatly reduced when attempted suicides are included in the statistics, believed to be a result of men using more violent or extreme – and thus, deadlier – methods. Even after all of this is accounted for, the 3:1 ratio is still immensely worrying. Suicide is arguably the most destructive symptom of toxic masculinity and the one in most need of attention.

Words can be more powerful than we anticipate

In the age of the internet and ISIS, we're exposed from a very young age to constant terror, graphic violence and an overwhelming sense that everything's a bit fucked really. Nothing shocks us anymore, we're hardened, desensitised. Knowing that, it can be easy to underestimate the power of words like 'boys don't cry' – it's just a throwaway phrase, right? Kids see videos of beheadings, and we're here worrying that a tired, old cliché is what's going to screw them up? Maybe it is a bit of a stretch, maybe 'boys don't cry' is trivial in the grand scheme of things, but even if the words themselves can be shrugged off, there is an immense weight behind them which we have to address. Of all the concerns facing men and masculinity right now, none are in need of more urgent attention than male suicide. I say that as the author of a book dealing with a broad range of such issues, and though I believe other areas are equally important to address on a long-term basis, our short-term priority ought to lie in reducing the number of men who take their own lives.

A few days before Christmas 2014, Jonny Sharples got a phone call telling him his older brother Simon had died. Simon, a 36-year-old father of one, had taken his own life. I was drawn to Simon and Jonny's story for pretty much the opposite reason you would expect, and wanted to tell it here not because it's a particularly extraordinary or unusual tale, but because it's the *very opposite* of that.

'On the surface, and I say this as somebody that loved my brother dearly, Simon was completely unremarkable. He was just a "normal" man; he was 36 years old when he passed away and I suppose he completely fitted into the stereotype of what you'd expect a 36-year-old man to be like.

'He was a very caring person too, I do think he found it diffi- cult to express his emotions sometimes – both the good and the not so good – but there was a person there who had a lot of love and care for people. From a personal point of view, I thought he may struggle to adapt to fatherhood when it happened back in 2011, but I think it's something he really relished. There was a wonderful bond between my brother and my nephew and that's apparent on photographs of them together. He really took to the role and the responsibility and I know the both of them had a lot of fun in one another's company.'

When I asked Jonny to tell me about Simon, I was almost surprised at how utterly mundane he made his brother sound, and the more I thought about it, the more I found this description quietly terrifying. Who among us doesn't know a man, several men, who resemble Simon closely? As someone who hasn't lost anyone from their immediate family or friendship group to suicide, I think it highlighted just how vulnerable to this I could be, how it could happen to literally anyone with little warning. One thing that impressed me about Jonny was his writing on the subject so soon after it happened, and his ability to keep a clear head and fight the good fight. He told me that there's still a lot of stigma around suicide and that it continues to be misunderstood by a lot of people.

'I have spoken to people, third parties who have seen other members of their family left behind by suicide, who say that they know people who want to brush it under the carpet and pretend that their loved one died in a different manner so it seems that stigma and public perception doesn't just have an impact on those who take their own lives but on others too. I think that's worrying as well, and just means there are more people out there who are struggling to come to terms with this and who need to help (and need help) in creating an environment we can all be comfortable in.'

The only time Jonny encountered any real resistance to open, positive conversations about suicide was in February 2015. The *Royle Family* actor Ralf Little had taken to Twitter to criticise footballer Clarke Carlisle over several issues, including a drink-driving incident, but also Carlisle's mental health and suicide attempts (about which Little accused Carlisle of 'not telling the full story' after an interview with the footballer was published in *The Sun*). Jonny wrote an open letter to Little over the tweets, which he said 'only seek to reinforce' the stigma surrounding suicide. To Little's credit, he shared Jonny's letter with his followers.

'Little himself seemed happy to be educated on the matter, he called it a considered reply, but many of his followers who then read it went down the route of calling suicide a selfish act and saying that depression is no excuse to behave in certain ways. That came a month and a half after Simon took his own life, and the open letter was only the second time I'd written about it. The first [published on a personal blog] was well received, so I was reasonably taken aback by some of the responses I got but I know that stigma is there and the only way to try to get rid of it is to face it head on. Other than that, people have been very receptive to the discussion – people often send me messages telling me their stories and about how my speaking about it has resonated with them. In speaking about it so publicly, and facing it head on, hopefully more people will do the same and help improve understanding around such an important issue.'

I also asked him if in some respect the social stigma towards suicide itself could actually increase the risk of suicidal thoughts in someone who feels unable to reach out for help.

'I think the stigma doesn't help, I think that no matter how much people are coming to terms with mental health in men and wanting to create the safe environment for men to talk, there still needs to be more done and I think that could take some time. There is certainly something stopping men coming forward and opening up, and in order to improve the chances of that happening then the stigma in society needs to be removed and men need to know that there's places for them to turn and it's okay for them to talk.'

You don't have to look at Jonny's Twitter account for long before it becomes clear what a big part of his life football is, and how important the community of friends he's made through the sport is. Shortly before we spoke, the male mental health awareness charity CALM – Campaign Against Living Miserably – teamed up with men's body spray titans Lynx (that's Axe to anyone outside of Britain) on a new campaign. Lynx is notorious for its advertisements, which critics have claimed are sexist and reinforce unhealthy notions of what masculinity is supposed to look like, so the partnership inevitably came under fire. It's not just the advertising that does this either, a New Yorker piece[15] about experimental psychologist Charles Spence revealed that:

In 2006, with funding from Unilever, Spence conducted a study to see whether altering the volume and pitch of the sound from an aerosol can would affect how a person perceives the pleasantness or forcefulness of a deodorant. Based on Spence's findings, the company invested in a packaging redesign for Axe deodorant, complete with new nozzle technology. The underarm spray, which is targeted at young men, now sounds noticeably louder than the company's gentler, female-targeted Dove brand.

CALM defended their partnership and said it was exactly because of the market Lynx reaches that they were a smart choice. Similarly, because of football's close association with masculinity (sometimes in a fairly toxic form), I was curious about what Jonny thought such a popular, uniting interest could do for something as devastating as the male suicide rate.

'I think there is so much that football can do for mental health, in the same way that Lynx had a readymade demographic for mental health campaigning – football has the same demographic and an even bigger reach. Football puts its weight behind a lot of worthwhile causes such as Prostate Cancer UK, Movember, etc. but it's rare that you will see them be so open with their support for mental health work, though it's clearly something that has an effect on football and on footballers. [The footballers] Robert Enke and Gary Speed both took their own lives in recent years, Clarke Carlisle has spoken out about his mental health, but there still needs to be more done and I believe football can help break down a lot of those barriers and end the stigma.'

Jonny is adamant that better education on the subject is needed in schools, while adults should be targeted by more campaigns (like those for which CALM are responsible). It seems, however, that one of the most effective ways of reaching men is through other men. The story of business analyst Geoff Lamb is testament to the power of male bonding and one of the clearest examples I've seen yet of why we should try to be more open with our mental health problems – not just for our sake, but for the sake of others too. During a stressful period at work, Lamb found his social life suffering: he was becoming more irritable and cancelling engagements at short notice. He finally dragged himself out to a gig with his mates at Wembley Arena to see Steel Panther (who he notes are 'pretty much a parody of toxic masculinity themselves') primarily because their support act Skindred are one of his all-time favourite live bands. After a few drinks in the pub and some issues getting into the venue, Lamb went ahead to catch the openers while his friends hung back at the bar.

'When they came & found me I wasn't at the front, I was standing at the back not getting into it at all. One of my friends realised that something was up, and it wasn't the band, or the venue organisers or any of the issues we'd been dealing with today. He'd been through a bit of a breakdown himself after breaking up with his long-term partner & he was seeing something of himself in my actions so he asked me if I was OK. I said "I'm really not, can we go somewhere quiet & talk about it?" We found a spot by the fire escape where we could hear each other's conversation and then I just broke down. I don't remember that much about the next hour or so but I basically spent it hugging my mate & sobbing hysterically – to the point his t-shirt was soaked through with my tears – while he hugged me back and told me it was going to be OK. I heartily recommend hugs by the way, they're the best. He gave me the time I needed and the literal shoulder to cry on, then made sure I got home OK, and explained to my mates what had happened and why I was no longer at the gig. He also gave me the phone number of his psychiatrist and spent the next few weeks texting me pretty much constantly to make sure I was OK and engage me in conversation.

'I ended up going through my health insurance at work instead of using the psychiatrist he recommended, and one of the first things I did was talk to my boss and tell her actually I'm not OK – at this point I was still assuming it was depression not anxiety. She was really supportive and has basically spent the whole year focusing on making sure I get well and making loads of accommodations for me to work flexibly around therapy etc. Now at work we have a lot of mental health awareness posters up featuring employees – always women – talking about their depression or similar things as part of a campaign to remove the stigma around mental illness. Buoyed by this, I decided I'd not hide what I was going through & mentioned to my colleagues what was going on and apologised for if I had been snappy with them. Shortly after this I get a phone call from one of my colleagues where he was quietly asking questions like "so is the therapy working for you?" and that sort of thing. So I asked if anything was up with him and he started opening up about how he was getting really stressed at work and going out binge drinking on the weekend to try to cope with it via a work hard/play hard sort of mind set. He was basically running on coffee and cigarettes all week while he pulled 12 hours a day, then getting tanked up at the weekend. He talked about how his dad had brought him up with what he called a "traditional Yorkshire" upbringing which basically boiled down to learning "boys don't cry, feelings are something girls have and if you think you have it hard in your heated air conditioned office let me tell you what it was like working down t' pit".

'So he was very uncomfortable talking to his friends or family about how he was struggling to cope because he was worried they'd think he was a bit of a sissy but he was comfortable talking to me because I had admitted I was in the same boat. So all it took to let this guy realise it was OK to ask for help was another guy admitting that he was getting therapy and taking medication. I was struck by how much that mirrored my experience with a friend giving me the number of his therapist causing me to go talk to my GP and my health insurer and since then I have been trying to be open and talk about mental health a lot more and never shied away from admitting I suffer from anxiety.

'I also found out later from my mum that before I was born my dad went through a period where he had a minor breakdown himself, and his GP prescribed the radical, new (at the time) technique of Conversation Based Therapy. It makes me wonder how much sooner I would have gone to the GP myself had my father had a frank discussion with me when I was younger about his own experiences with therapy. To date my father has still said nothing on the subject despite me talking to him about my medication and therapy.'

It's that last paragraph that really gets to me in Lamb's story and shows how far we still have to go. Even someone who has struggled with anxiety and depression, and knows his son does too, feels unable to bring up the subject. This is exactly why we need to tackle this from as early on as possible.

Where to begin?

As long as it's the norm to dress boys in blue and girls in pink, we will continue to perpetuate the absurd idea that literally anything, physical or abstract – be it a colour, a hobby or a personality trait – can be inherently and exclusively linked to one gender. To impose this so ubiquitously on beings whose abilities are limited to crying, drinking, pissing and shitting (or what I call 'Friday night', but seriously...) serves only to further the narrative that gender is not an identity constructed by an individual, but a fixed social concept to which we must adhere. I haven't even touched upon how this affects trans people yet (something I'll address in more detail later on), but if you can see that being forced to comply with certain expectations of gender is harmful to cis people, just *think* what it's doing to those whose gender doesn't match the sex they were assigned at birth.

Unless we as a society refuse to accept that blue is for boys and pink is for girls, we've already lost the war. As children grow older, there is at least some opportunity for them to make personal choices, however much these may be influenced by society, but babies have no say whatsoever. And while they personally aren't aware of what this means, it sends a message to everyone else that this is how it should be, and influences the actions of others. If the majority of parents feel they should dress their babies according to sex, then it's safe to assume that the majority of parents believe their child should conform to a rigid set of ideals according to gender.

I'm not saying that gender-neutral clothes will bring about a revolution in our attitudes overnight, but they would make a difference. As visibility increases and retailers start to evolve, the mere fact that an option exists is enough to encourage critical thought on the subject. If parents can feel that it's okay to dress their baby however they want, then maybe they can accept that the same thing applies to how their child acts. When the world is telling you there are right or wrong ways to be a certain gender, it's easy to get sucked into that belief yourself, but with a little less pressure and a little more freedom, change can happen.

If boys can wear pink, then why can't they cry?

I set out to write this book not as an attack on masculinity itself, but on the corrupted values with which it has become synonymous. For the most part, the traits we have traditionally encouraged men to aspire to are nothing short of admirable, it's just that somewhere down the line we became detached from the complex reality of these, started to oversimplify them or believe we could take shortcuts in order to achieve what was desired. 'Boys don't cry' is a mentality that was obviously born out of strength, of which – as both a physical and philosophical concept – the association with masculinity is as old as time itself. Strength and bravery are at the very core of self-preservation, prized as much today as in the caves, beneficial in every imaginable part of our lives. When it's time to step up, what could possibly look less strong than crying? It's the ultimate display of weakness and resignation, more so than even the defeat itself, and there absolutely are times when it's important for us to be able to hold back the tears: we may have been beaten, but through refusing to concede and admit our opponents have won, we can retain power, pride and dignity by denying them what they want to see – not just for ourselves, but for those around us.

But while it may prove beneficial in these particular situations, there are plenty of times when the catharsis of crying – or an equivalent means of venting – is necessary, and nothing to do with staying strong in the face of our enemies. It's hard to say if this is an entirely modern problem, but worth noting that Odysseus and his men – paragons of Ancient Greek masculinity – cried openly and without hesitation, suggesting that not crying wasn't always the show of strength it's often considered to be nowadays. Based on what we know about how men deal with their mental health, I don't think anyone can deny that the inability to properly express our emotions is having a major effect on our well-being, and for the worse. In some extreme cases, men's families have known nothing about what they're dealing with until it's too late, forced to question if things might have turned out differently had they been aware. Indeed, though my father's illness was physical, the way he dealt with it in total solitude was very much the same, and had my mother known, he almost certainly wouldn't have evaded medical consultation as he did. Crying is seen as a weakness because it reveals our true emotions and leaves us exposed to further defeat; by hiding the extent of how we feel, if nothing else we can walk away with our heads held high. In a culture that teaches men this, it is no shock whatsoever that they quite literally guard their emotions with their life. Were it a desirable trait of masculinity to repress your feelings and keep your loved ones from ever finding out, then this would be a resounding success! But try to remember the ultimate goal that we're pursuing here. While definitions may vary from one man to the next, if something's responsible for your inevitable destruction I wouldn't be inclined to call that a strength.

I started this chapter talking about baby clothes and ended on suicide, which I suppose is a bit like someone taking you to a poultry farm to pet the cutest, fluffiest chicks before leading you into the barn of battery hens and then on to the mechanical slaughterhouse. It probably wasn't the easiest thing to deal with emotionally so, uh, sorry about that, but I'm sure we can all agree it's been quite the ride! On a more serious note, I did have my reasons for this. I'm not actually blaming baby clothes for the high rate of male suicide (at least not in quite so direct terms) but these things may be more closely connected than you think. It's all part of a wider culture surrounding gender, fuelled by innumerable factors which are deeply embedded within society, and no single product or attitude or phrase can be expected to shoulder more blame than anything else. I decided to focus on baby clothes though, because they're pretty much the first thing we introduce into a person's life to differentiate them based on their assigned gender in an utterly arbitrary and unnecessary way. As long as it's the norm to dress babies in gender-appropriate clothes, we are saying that gender is absolute, and that the way we present it to the world can be considered in such simplified terms as right and wrong. If we're willing to accept that baby boys should wear blue, then we're willing to accept there are other things males should or shouldn't do based on their gender.

Humans for the most part are sheep: our attitudes are easily swayed by those around us because we have an inherent desire to conform. If all parents suddenly stopped dressing babies in gender-appropriate clothes, you're obviously not going to see a plummet in the male suicide rate, but honestly, any step we take away from the idea that there are right or wrong ways for males to behave, is a step in the right direction. It *will* prompt people to ask questions and think a bit more critically about both their own actions and those they encourage in others. 'Boys don't cry' may seem insignificant, but it feeds into the idea that men should not express any emotion, and at its most extreme, this attitude is literally killing us. Just one less voice in the world telling a young man he's not allowed to cry and one more saying it's okay to talk about feelings can make a big difference. And if we can make these small changes, bit by bit, over time, it may just start saving lives.

Fight Club: Aggression, Risk and Mob Mentality

When I first wrote about the circumstances of my dad's death, I spent a while contemplating some strong counterpoints to my argument. I was certain masculinity had played a large role in his premature death, and to this day I still believe that had he been less guarded we may not have lost him so early. But even with overwhelming evidence to back this up, it was at odds with the image I had of Richard Urwin, pieced together from ever-fading memories, photos, home videos and the anecdotes other people told.

I could not stop fixating on the absurdity that was the description of my father as 'masculine'. If you'd ever met the guy, you'd know exactly what I mean. He was not a lad's lad, that's for sure. He took little interest in most sport and didn't present himself as outwardly macho in the things he said or how he carried himself. I must stress, none of this is a criticism in any way – Christ knows, I've largely followed in his footsteps. And then there's the matter of those fucking lycra cycling shorts I mentioned earlier. Forgive the perhaps outdated stereotyping, but skin-tight, wet-look, to-all-intents-and-purposes hotpants *hardly* scream of one's rampant status as an alpha male, do they?

Because of this, it felt very odd indeed to be preaching about how this ostensibly unmasculine man was a victim of his own hypermasculinity. However, this really isn't uncommon. Indeed, when we look at how masculinity affects men's health, we tend to perceive this as something passive, as what men *aren't* doing; when men fail to seek help for legitimate medical concerns, or find themselves unable to discuss emotional issues it can have devastating consequences. As we have already established, there are endless tragic stories of men who have taken their own lives, revealing to their often unsuspecting families the unspoken pain with which they had lived. Silence is, by its very nature, passive, and it's true that this is most often the focus of campaigns that are geared towards the gender.

This is fascinating to me, though, as I think to most people the definition of 'masculine' is aligned with a very different image: one of lad culture, strength, power and, often, intolerable sexist pricks down the pub. This macho state, which one might refer to as *active* masculinity, is a far cry from that which killed my father – but in its own loud, explosive manner, it can be just as deadly as silence.

There's an odd sort of dichotomy at play in our perceptions of active versus passive masculinity. For several years now, Samaritans (a charity dedicated to providing support to those in emotional distress or at risk of suicide) has run a campaign with particular visibility inside railway stations and other suicide hotspots. The series of 'We're in your corner' posters depict men in traditionally masculine roles with appropriately-worded copy such as 'A Samaritan helped me find my strength'.

In the research stage of the campaign, the Samaritans tested four different potential characters: a boxing trainer, a soldier, a musician and a rugby player. Reactions to the first two were overwhelmingly positive, as 'boxing remains a tough, well-respected, accessible sport among working class men' while 'the soldier character garnered respect, and it was acknowledged that he could have potentially "seen things" that could cause him to have problems'. Reactions to the rugby player were neutral, but negative towards the musician (he was perceived as having problems entirely of his own making, so people were largely unsympathetic towards his plight). The final run of posters used the boxing trainer and soldier, and added a third character: a physical labourer in hi-vis worksite clothes. The Samaritans' characters and their reasons behind their choices offered up some revealing insights into how men see mental health and masculinity, suggesting that in order to successfully prevent male suicide – or at least open up dialogue on the subject – men need to accept that traditionally macho characters can suffer these problems and that it's not a sign of weakness to ask for help.

Unfortunately, this sort of thinking, while common, can be immensely destructive. I cannot fault the Samaritans for attempting to prevent suicide (and you'd be nothing short of a bastard to do so) but this campaign is symptomatic of a wider problem in society. What the Samaritans seem to be saying is 'it's not emasculating to need help', and while this is of course true, it's loaded with a whole host of dodgy connotations. At best, this campaign is a very short-term solution, and while absolutely anything that reduces the number of people taking their own lives should be commended, we need to look into how this thinking affects the future. My main problem is that the posters reinforce the idea that masculinity is something to strive towards, rather than telling men 'honestly, it doesn't fucking matter if you're a soldier or if you do some other job that people don't consider masculine'. Over time, campaigns like these continue this socially-constructed idea of The Ideal Man and a specific gender binary, which alienates anyone who doesn't conform absolutely.

This is in no way the fault of the Samaritans, but that of society – the Samaritans are fighting for a vital cause with admirable effort. Wouldn't it be great, though, if rather than telling men that it wasn't emasculating to ask for help, we told them that emasculation itself wasn't actually a thing? If we showed men that these perceptions of gender in the first place were total bullshit?

The sad fact is that the way we behave in our attempts to be seen as masculine are often just as deadly as our inability when it comes to emotional communication. Suicide only recently overtook traffic accidents as the leading cause of death in British men under 35 years old; and the number of lives taken on the country's roads highlights a different sort of toxic masculinity in itself.

At the end of 2012, the European Court of Justice began enforcing a ban against insurance companies discriminating on the basis of gender when it came to setting premiums for customers. It was a notably rare incident of women coming out worse from anti-gender discrimination laws, which, historically speaking, have been geared towards improving their lives and giving them much-needed support in a viciously patriarchal world. This time around, though, the law meant that costs were forced up for women, particularly with regard to motoring insurance.

In order to achieve true equality, this sort of legislation is necessary, but in that situation it seemed like a weird move. After all, women *are* safer drivers and there's loads of evidence to back this up. The reason for the disparity in premiums previous to the 2012 ban was founded on the very simple truth that a woman is much less likely than a man to be involved in an accident resulting in insurance claims. Regardless of your opinion on whether insurers should be given the freedom to charge women less, this does bring to light the issue of safety and risk. Men, of course, have the ability to drive as safely as women, and everyone, regardless of gender, takes the same test in order to prove their diligence behind the wheel. Why, then, are men more likely to crash?

If you put me in the passenger seat of a car being driven by a woman, I tend to feel much safer with her than if the car is being driven by a man, particularly a young man. The statistics seem to justify my fears: in the UK, the average number of men killed or seriously injured behind the wheel of a car in any given year is more than twice that of women.[16] I don't know exactly why men drive more dangerously, but they do seem to get a kick out of it. Unlike women, young men often seem to have something to prove, and if there are passengers in the car then you're far more likely to see this machismo come into play. Whether it's for this reason above all others I don't know, but how often have you heard people attributing speedy or unsafe driving to 'overcompensation'? You've probably worked out that I am, in a none-too-subtle way, referring to dick size. 'Men aren't driving dangerously because they're worried what people think about their schlong,' you say. I beg to differ.

In the latter part of last decade, a road safety campaign in the Australian state of New South Wales featured images of women waving their pinkie fingers at young men who sped past, with the slogan 'Speeding: No One Thinks Big Of You'. The premise was clear and to the point: if you drive unsafely, people assume your penis is small. It was a novel approach to the subject but one of such brilliant simplicity you were left wondering why it had taken so long for an ad agency to tap into this mindset. It was a totally different tactic following years of graphic imagery showing the bloody consequences of driving. And what's most important is that it seemed to show genuinely promising results, with fewer road deaths being reported after the first year and three quarters of young drivers in the region saying the adverts had encouraged them to stick to the limit.

Leigh Bignell of Ogilvy – one of the largest marketing companies in the world – commented that the campaign worked on drivers because 'they were more scared of being uncool than dying'[17], which is of course true. But on a deeper level, it was effective because Clemenger BBDO, the agency responsible, were able to identify why young men were driving unsafely, and then take this very concept and rip it to shreds in a way that was as entertaining as it was effective. No, a man's worth is not defined by the size of his genitals, and as we're told time and again, this isn't a measure of one's sexual ability – but plenty of men whether consciously or not do believe otherwise, and the fear of other people (for hetero men this especially means women) perceiving them as having tiny todgers is, remarkably, enough to effect a significant attitudinal change.

Risk, it seems, is perceived as a masculine trait. But where does this come from? Consider the fact that *Top Gear* is the most widely watched factual programme in the world and perhaps the reasons for this behaviour aren't so mysterious. In the interests of full disclosure, I should state for the record that I am not a fan of *Top Gear*; not that there's any ambiguity in what I'm about to say, but if it all seems very biased then that's just because I detest the programme and think its presenters are some of the worst living humans-who-haven't-actually-murdered-or-raped-or-enslaved-anyone. That doesn't mean you shouldn't listen to what I have to say about it, though.

Young men are particularly impressionable, and are taught by cultural institutions such as *Top Gear* that dangerous behaviour is both 'manly' and something to be rewarded. As the comedian Stewart Lee says, *Top Gear* presenter Richard Hammond is someone who 'carved a best-selling literary career off the back of his own inability to drive safely'. While I am loathe to suggest a clear link between the programme and bad driving (if only because I fear my premature descent into middle age and the inevitable 'video games cause violence' rants that are sure to follow) I do think shows like this can have an extraordinary effect on the minds of young men.

I say young men, because that's the demographic I believe is most susceptible. Look at the three men who (until very recently) presented the show, and at their laddish jokes that often carry undertones of homophobia or suggestions of one another's effeminacy. The way they spur each other on to commit foolish tasks is practically *identical* to the kind of peer pressure that makes so many young lives utterly miserable. Like it or not, Clarkson, May and Hammond are role models for young men, and when your role models are paid millions to drive cars fast, that's probably going to factor into your own decisions.

If you don't believe the impressive power over people's thoughts and emotions shows like *Top Gear* have, then you probably didn't pay that much attention to the uproar that accompanied the BBC's firing of the show's head honcho Jeremy Clarkson. After Clarkson was initially suspended for (allegedly) punching a producer in the face, more than a million living, breathing, sentient human beings leapt to his defence, signing a petition calling for his immediate reinstatement, with plenty of what were presumably the same people abusing any-one on social media who dared voice a perfectly reasonable stance opposing this unpleasant act. For these people, the fact Clarkson had assaulted a co-worker supposedly because a hot meal hadn't been provided, was not an issue; they put it down to a 'boys will be boys' mentality. That right there is your problem. The pro-Clarkson brigade argued it was perfectly normal behav-iour for one man to physically assault another in the workplace, which brings me to perhaps the most despicable aspect of active masculinity: violence. Such is the ubiquity of male violence that many of us are now depressingly desensitised to it, and it feels like it comes as part and parcel in any event or place where large groups of men tend to congregate.

The most obvious example of this is in sport, which in Britain, more often than not, translates to football. I must admit that right now, in 2015, football has a fairly good reputation for safety, but it wasn't always this way.

With their origins in the 1960s, by the time the '70s rolled around squads of organised hooligans were attached to the fan-bases of a good portion of Britain's larger football teams, and by the '80s and '90s hooliganism in British football had become so notorious that it was a frequent source of material for pop culture across the world.

In Bill Hicks' 1992 stand-up excerpt *The War*, he draws attention to the disparity in gun-related deaths in Britain and the US: fourteen versus roughly 23,000 in the previous year, but adds:

'Okay, though, admittedly, last year in England, they had fourteen thousand deaths per every soccer game, okay. I'm not saying every system is flawless, I'm just saying, if you're in England, don't go to a goddamn soccer game.' By the late '90s, hooliganism had been all but eradicated from British football, but its association with the sport (and by extension the country) was still deeply embedded in the global conscience. A 1997 episode of *The Simpsons*, 'The Cartridge Family', began with the family's first trip to a soccer match devolving into violence, the whole town soon falling victim to riots that started off the back of the game.

If you were to come into the conversation knowing absolutely nothing about football or its violent history, and someone gave you a brief background into hooliganism, but no details as to who the perpetrators were, I would be *astounded* if you assumed the hooligan population was anything other than vastly male because, on a large-scale basis, women just don't have that same violent streak that men do.

In 2011, Turkey's football association trialled drastic measures against clubs who had been sanctioned for violence, with the Istanbul-based team Fenerbahçe being ordered to play two home matches without any spectators. However, they relaxed the rules to instead ban men from attending games and to allow in women and children for free. The Telegraph noted that the 'visiting team was greeted with applause, instead of the usual jeering', with their midfielder Omer Aysan quoted as saying, 'It was such a fun and pleasant atmosphere'[18]. Remove the men and: well, things do get nicer.

There has been a backlash against the shitty atmosphere that men create in these environments, and I became interested in small-time football fanatics the Clapton Ultras for precisely this reason. Hardcore supporters of the East London, non-league club Clapton FC, the Clapton Ultras not only attempt to bring football back to the working class, but also have their roots in the antifascist movement, rallying against racism, homophobia and violence in all its forms. In December 2014 Steve Hedley, assistant general secretary of the RMT union, was challenged at the ground over allegations that he was guilty of domestic violence. He was excluded by the Clapton Ultras, but later returned to the ground with allies, resulting in the verbal and physical assaults of several women. The Ultras hit out at Hedley's behaviour on their website, reaffirming the need for a safe, welcoming environment for all. Within the post, they decried the 'patriarchal aggression' still prevalent within football and linked to a report published by the Scottish Centre for Crime and Justice Research, exploring how domestic violence regularly spikes on match days. It highlighted that, in this form, the harmful effects of masculinity are felt by a much wider population than merely men themselves.

It's unfair to suggest football is the only sport in which violence is a problem, of course. There is an often spoken adage along the lines of 'football is a gentleman's sport played by thugs; rugby is a thug's sport played by gentlemen', which is both fairly classist and wrong. While rugby may not have the same history of violence perpetrated by fans as football, if you've witnessed the antics of rugby clubs in any students' union up and down the country, you will know the vile, shitting-in-pint-glasses, rape-culture-perpetuating behaviour 'rugby lads' are guilty of. Catch them on their own and they'll probably come off looking like decent members of society, but together there exists a mob mentality among men that's characterised by excess on all levels.

Indeed, it's unfair to suggest the problem is inherently related to any sport – it just happens to be exacerbated by the fact that most popular sports involve gatherings of large groups of men. The same is true of music, and though as a huge music fan it pains me to say it, I fear music may actually have a harder time accepting this truth. In 2014, Alanna McArdle, singer of (the absolutely fantastic) punk band Joanna Gruesome, hit out at the mosh pits where she'd witnessed fans injuring and endangering people (particularly women) at her band's shows, describing the culture as 'a macho and archaic throwback'[19]. Alongside sexual harassment and groping, the violence and unconsenting nature of mosh pits are further reasons why many women feel so unsafe in live music venues. To all intents and purposes, this is lad culture at its most toxic and any outsider who isn't prepared to conform with its awful, hyper-masculine bullshit is treated with hostility. Music should not be like this, and punk music in particular has a proud history of opposing prejudice in all its forms (well, apart from the neo-Nazi scene that spawned the likes of Skrewdriver; and the less said about that the better), but the fact is, violence of a sexual or otherwise nature is a trope of modern music, and in fact just about any environment that hosts men en masse.

Even in fiction, the link between masculinity and aggression is drawn time and time again. Take that bastion of cultural knowledge beloved of every 17-year-old boy, *Fight Club*. Although I'll happily admit to enjoying both Chuck Palahniuk's novel and David Fincher's adaptation, I do think its merits as a meaningful exploration into masculinity are not quite as explosive as some young men (my teenage self included) might have you believe. However, that *Fight Club* has such a big place in the hearts of many men suggests that its themes carry some sort of significance which I believe it's worth investigating, especially when you consider the numerous incidences since its release of copycat clubs inspired by the film or book. You can argue that those involved were missing the point, but it highlighted the fact that this idea of physical violence being inextricably linked to masculinity resonated with a lot of men. By which I mean: *Fight Club* as a work of art may not have anything meaningful to teach us, but its impact may.

'We're a generation of men raised by women', *Fight Club*'s Tyler Durden says, decrying the masculinity we lost as a result of having absent fathers, and justifying the need to fight as a means of reclaiming this. In the book, the eponymous fight clubs become a sort of replacement for traditional means of therapy for many of their participants, all of whom are disillusioned young men. Yes, it's a commentary on capitalism and advertising and that whole weird decade that was the 1990s. Yes, it's fictional. But the theme of large groups of men gathering and focusing their masculinity into something violent and, through Project Mayhem*, ultimately destructive, is all too familiar. And like I said, the real-life fight clubs spawned by the book's existence reflect this idea that men see violence and masculinity as synonymous. If we remove the idea of fight clubs from their beginnings in *Fight Club*, how different are they to sports such as boxing? Boxing being the very same sport that the Samaritans deemed manly enough to be used in a campaign encouraging men to believe that seeking help was not emasculating? The common themes that link this sort of dystopian fiction, driving, sport, music, and any cultural institution in which men gather, are: danger, violence and, above all, unnecessary risk.

Risk is such an interesting trait to be linked to masculinity. While violence can sometimes be explained by a mob mentality, accidents resulting from careless risk-taking seem to happen regardless of whether men are in groups or alone. When people look at the gender disparity in deaths caused by accidents at

* The anti-corporate organisation whose aim is to attack the materialist western world through acts of vandalism e.g. attempting to push a boulder-like sculpture downhill into a Starbucks. In the final scene of *Fight Club*, all the skyscrapers in the city housing credit card records are demolished by explosives Project Mayhem planted, their aim being to destroy the records and erase all personal debt.

work, the point is often raised that men are far more likely to work as physical labourers, thus vastly increasing their risk of injury as a result of factors such as falls or mishandling heavy machinery. This would certainly make sense when accounting for death or serious injury in the workplace, but it isn't that simple; we're not killing ourselves exclusively during the hours of 9 to 5. Once more you could point to the fact that men possibly do more DIY or physical tasks than women, but there's also a tendency towards riskier behaviour that seems almost as if it's embedded deeply within the Y chromosome.

When I was about 11 years old, I remember a friend and myself having an unfathomable amount of fun in reading up on the Darwin Awards which, if you're unfamiliar, collect reports of people who have mistakenly killed themselves in outlandishly foolish, unusual and entertaining ways, or otherwise eliminated themselves from the gene pool by 'self-sterilisation'*. (As a side note, that's fairly dark humour for an 11-year old when I consider it in retrospect, but as I stated in the introduction that was sort of my thing.) In 2014, the awards celebrated two decades of existence with the news that roughly 90% of its winners were male. Whatever justifiable reasons you can suggest for this disparity it's pretty fucking hard to account for a gender gap *quite* that enormous.

Researchers have pointed to what they call Male Idiot Theory (MIT) for the gap[20], and that's the actual term they used in the British Medical Journal, so I have no hesitations about using it

---

* This is the Darwin Awards' oddly conservative choice of words for what generally translates to 'serious trauma to the genitals, rendering the subject unable to reproduce'.

here because it's clearly very real. There hasn't been a great deal of research into MIT, but scientists have said there is anecdotal evidence (such as the Darwin Awards) to suggest its existence. As explained by the *Daily Mail*:

> Writing in the *British Medical Journal*, the researchers said it is puzzling men are willing to take such unnecessary risks – simply as a rite of passage, in pursuit of male social esteem or solely in exchange for 'bragging rights'.
>
> Dr Dennis Lendrem, of the University of Newcastle, said: 'Idiotic risks are defined as senseless risks, where the apparent payoff is negligible or non-existent, and the outcome is often extremely negative and often final.
>
> 'According to "male idiot theory" (MIT) many of the differences in risk-seeking behaviour, emergency department admissions, and mortality may be explained by the observation that men are idiots and idiots do stupid things.'

The real question we have to ask (not so much about MIT itself as about violence, aggression, risk, dangerous behaviour and all this shit associated with manhood) is one involving nature versus nurture.

Evolutionary Neuroandrogenic (ENA) theory explores the idea that testosterone is responsible for increased levels of aggression, and as the dominant sex hormone present in men, goes some way to explaining why we're much more likely to be involved in crime, particularly violent crime, than women are. However, it's all pretty loosely linked and there's no conclusive evidence to suggest higher levels of testosterone are a cause of aggressive behaviour. In my unscientific opinion, I also have a problem with people drawing links such as these as I fear they are all too often used to justify the awful behaviour of men and boys, ignoring the much greater issue of how we are brought up and socialised to act. I think it's incredibly rare for a man raised in a stable, happy and caring family from birth to become a violent or aggressive adult, and I firmly believe that these qualities, like any personality flaws, are learned.

As an adolescent in a state school, I saw with my own eyes on a weekly, sometimes daily, basis the way a fight between two boys in a playground could break out: a few choice words and warning pushes at the beginning, but things would generally only heat up after a small crowd had formed, encircling the pair, the shouts of 'FIGHT! FIGHT! FIGHT! FIGHT!' being a call to bring in a bigger audience. The human tendency towards self-preservation is strong enough that without their peers in attendance, most of the time such an incident would result in one or both of the parties walking away unscathed. As someone who has been punched in the face twice in his life, I can tell you: the desire to not be punched in the face will override pretty much any other thought or emotion when faced with a situation in which you may be punched in the face. But once a few dozen others have joined you, you're on an enclosed stage. Everyone is telling you to fight, and while walking away will save you physical pain, the humiliation you'll face will probably leave deeper scars in the long-term. And so you go for it, even though every fucking bit of good sense in your body is screaming at you to run.

In a way, it's a bit like that reaction to the Australian road safety ad: you're more afraid of being uncool than, well, getting punched in the face. Walking away, with a crowd of dozens of young men watching, means feeling like you're less of a man. Some people say adolescents fight because they're hormonal, giving credence to the ENA theory, but I have little doubt that adolescents fight because of social conditioning. When you're 13, 15, 18, the most important thing in the world is being as cool as possible, as much as I wish that wasn't the case. If you can impress your peers at that age, your entire life will be so much easier to live, and a lot of how you experience that age will shape your personality as an adult. So you do what you have to in order to be cool. Claim this behaviour is chemical all you like, but I ask that you consider this: if two boys exchange insults and there's no one around to witness the outcome, to spur them on, do you think they're more or less likely to resort to fists?

Men fear emasculation – perhaps more than anything else – so they do anything they can to ensure that the image they project to others is one of masculinity, and to reassure themselves of their own social standing as men. If someone comes along and proves me wrong, and can conclusively demonstrate that violence and aggression and risk and dangerous behaviour in men is all down to testosterone, then so be it. For now, I'll bet you every last penny in my bank account that if all men were taught emasculation wasn't something to fear, we'd have a much better world for everyone.

Man Down: Masculinity in the Military and Institutionalised Violence

Walk up to a complete stranger in pretty much any country, ask them 'what are some timeless, positive qualities associated with masculinity?' and it's fairly likely they'd ignore you, based on the fact you're a complete stranger and they probably don't speak English very well, and why would you do that? On the off-chance you do get a valid response and repeat the experiment enough times to build some kind of sample (again, what's wrong with you? Leave these people alone) you might start to see a pattern of words like 'courage', 'strength' and possibly 'loyalty'. Regardless of where in the world you are, there's seemingly a handful of timeless traits that humans consider to be desirable in men. If you did a similar survey, but this time changing the subject from men to soldiers, there's a high probability many of the answers will be the same. This is hardly a coincidence.

For as long as countries and borders and wars have existed, military and masculinity have been tied at the hip. I've already touched upon this connection – indeed, the first piece I ever wrote on the subject theorised that the two World Wars were directly responsible for a widespread change in the attitudes of men – but I believe it warrants a slightly more in-depth look; there is much we can learn about masculinity from this aspect of society. Curious to know what motivates a young man to join the military and how macho the atmosphere inside is, I talked to Josh Huddleston, a veteran of the US Marines who was deployed to Djibouti in 2004 and Iraq between 2005 and 2006.

'My father was a marine. He served one enlistment from '79 to '82 and always said he wished he would have stayed in for a full 20 years or more. He only got out because my mom wanted him to. Growing up, he would tell me stories about boot camp and life in the Corps and there was always something about it that appealed to me. When I was in junior high, I pretty much decided I'd be joining after high school. I played [American] football until high school, and then decided to run cross-country instead, to better prepare myself for the Marines and to avoid being permanently injured, had I continued to play football. It was also in high school that one of my best friends decided he'd join with me and we would go through boot camp together – by the end of high school, two other close friends in our circle also decided to join us.

'We would all watch war movies together and cheer on the violence, thinking there'd be no greater purpose or experience in life than that of suffering through combat. Movies are just one example, but this is where I feel a huge reason for me joining was almost certainly – though I obviously didn't know it at the time – the sum of all of American popular culture, which is sort of ruled by a deep-seated, oppressive machismo. I grew up in a rural part of Ohio, just across the Ohio River from Kentucky and West Virginia. It's a very traditional way of life. Guns are revered. Politically, the population is overwhelmingly conservative. Everyone goes to church. Growing up in that environment leads to lots of young boys eager to "serve their country". Another reason was my family was poor. If I joined up, not only would I get to experience the military, but I could also get a ton of money to go to college with afterward.

'And, of course, there's the fact I've always been a smaller fella. Growing up, I was self-conscious of it and felt pretty insecure. I never allowed myself to be bullied, probably because I have two older brothers of relatively close age who did their share of brotherly teasing and whatnot. I'm sure a lot could be said regarding masculinity about this fact alone, but my smaller stature definitely caused a feeling of inferiority. I felt "What better way to prove my manhood than by joining the toughest branch of the military? That'll get me respect." I joined the Delayed Entry Program (which lets you enlist at the end of your junior year of high school, to take a year off of your full 8-year commitment) three months before September 11th, 2001. 9/11 only intensified my desire to serve. By the time I graduated high school in May 2002, my dad's pain pill addiction was out of control and we were fighting in Afghanistan – Iraq wasn't on the radar yet. You couldn't have paid me a billion dollars to not join. I left for boot camp three days after graduation.'

It comes as little shock when he tells me that all branches of the military are dominated by an expectation of masculinity – and I think it's safe to say this is not exclusive to the United States – but the Marine Corps has something of a reputation even within the forces for its machismo and, in Josh's own words, 'any perception of weakness is rooted out and dealt with pretty quickly.

'I remember in boot camp, there was a recruit in my platoon who had very effeminate mannerisms. He couldn't "sound off", which is arguably the most important thing you can do in boot camp to keep from getting fucked with by the drill instructors (DIs). "Sounding off" in the context of the military is yelling as loudly as you possibly can. If you're not sounding off when the DIs address you, you get "quarterdecked", or taken aside and intensely exercised. Anyway, I remember this recruit disappeared one day. Our senior drill instructor said he got recycled, that he wasn't "hacking it", so he was sent to a new platoon to start over. I'm sure the intention was out of hopes he would quit during the first two or three days of his new cycle, which is permitted – even though they don't tell you until after those days have ended, probably for good reason, because most people would quit. A strong physicality is looked upon higher than just about everything else. In the eyes of many marines, a high PFT (Physical Fitness Test) score makes you a better marine than actually being good at your job.'

I've known Josh since before my first VICE article on the subject was published, and he confessed that up until then he hadn't realised toxic masculinity was as much of a problem in the UK as in his home country – partly because he believes American culture itself is so influential on young men in this respect.

'The military is the epitome of all things masculine that Americans are culturally bombarded with while growing up.

It starts with sports. We're encouraged, from a young age, to join a team and weekly "go to battle" on a field and crash our bodies into one another. The military is just an extension of this in the form of a much bigger team. We watch supposedly anti-war movies like *Saving Private Ryan* and think "Oh, it's so terrible what they had to go through. War is hell." And yet, there's an appeal to it with young, impressionable, teenage boys like myself. They end up being recruiting films, to an extent. First-person shooter video games always sell really well. Who doesn't love a good headshot in a video game? This shit all adds up and, perhaps subconsciously, makes young men eager for the possibility of having these experiences. The military is the obvious outlet.'

Until very recently, it was practically unheard of for anyone who wasn't a cisgender, heterosexual man to join the armed forces of pretty much any nation. Today, many restrictions still apply. Even in western countries we may consider to be more progressive: at the time of writing, British women are unable to serve on the frontline. In the United States, which prides itself on being the 'land of the free', the repeal of Don't Ask Don't Tell in 2011 allowed soldiers who were openly gay or bisexual to serve for the first time – for almost two decades before this, gay people were technically permitted but only on the condition that they kept their sexuality secret from their colleagues. But while the Obama administration's lifting of DADT was hailed as a victory for human rights, a ban on transgender people in the US military remains in place. The reason the American government lets this particular form of discrimination continue has its basis in the increasingly outdated idea that gender dysphoria (which is defined as 'the condition of feeling one's emotional and psychological identity as male or female to be opposite to one's biological sex') is a mental illness – much as homosexuality was once perceived to be – something that renders an individual unfit to serve.

However, it's becoming a lot harder for the US to justify this, as a growing number of trans people are serving openly in their allies' militaries. Since 1999, the British armed forces have allowed anyone regardless of gender or sexuality to apply, and alongside this have implemented strict rules regarding discrimination on any level. That's not to say the military hasn't seen its fair share of homophobia and transphobia, but due to the systems in place to deal with complaints of this nature and their zero tolerance approach, the army, navy and air force have all earned places in Stonewall's top 100 employers[21] for LGBT people. In Israel, national service is compulsory for all citizens over the age of 18 (with a handful of the usual exceptions), regardless of sex – though women serve two years and men serve three. Gay, lesbian and bisexual people are permitted to serve openly, and unlike in the US, gender dysphoria is not considered an exclusionary condition. In fact, the Israeli Defence Forces recognise that hormone replacement therapy, sex reassignment surgery and counselling can be medically necessary for transgender people, and can even pay for such treatment if required. Britain and Israel are two of the United States' strongest allies, meaning that American soldiers inevitably served alongside openly LGBT people from these countries before DADT was repealed and personally witnessed the lack of problems associated with such inclusivity – something which has given LGBT campaigners significant ammunition to use against the US. While the US has yet to catch up with its allies, this pressure does suggest there's hope for change in the not-too-distant future. There's a plethora of reasons why this would be an important, positive development, but I'm particularly intrigued by how it would affect one area that's less frequently discussed and, SURPRISE, it concerns masculinity.

Based on what I've previously written about war, as well as my general social and political leanings, you could quite fairly assume that my opinion of the military as an institution and the way it contributes to toxic behaviour in men is one that's conclusively partisan. This was the case for most of my socially aware life, and while my overall beliefs haven't changed in any major way, I have had to reevaluate some aspects of my understanding and admit that things aren't as black and white as I once thought.

The problem with the hard-left's view that the military as an institution, in and of itself, is harmful and should be dismantled as far as possible, is that it's such an unrealistic aim that it actually stands in the way of achieving positive changes. What I mean is: armed forces are an inevitability, but by writing them off on a grand scale, you're essentially giving up on trying to solve some of the inherent problems in the military. For starters, we have to ask why young men in particular are drawn to armed combat. It is not enough to say that the army, navy or air force encourage a culture of toxic masculinity without questioning the reasons behind this and what we can do to address it.

In 2014, I spoke to Christina Bentley shortly after she came out as the first transgender RAF police officer, an interview that opened my eyes to the power gender holds over our motives and made me realise why institutions such as the military can be so important.

'The idea was that I was trying to push myself out of myself, so I ended up joining the military and doing really well,' she says. 'I wanted to help people, but there was a background of "this is perceived as quite masculine", and it all masked who I am. I did stupid things to hide myself and I never needed to.'

After spending two years in the military, it was her first posting to the Qualified Police Dogs unit on the Falkland Islands and subsequent return that allowed her to get going on the path to self acceptance.

'The Falklands became my final push to get the woman out of me,' recalls Christina. 'I did all the boy stuff – I went drinking, I went to the gym every night. I ended up being about 86 kilos of muscle. I was a big boy. It was a good tour and I enjoyed it, but I didn't really have a chance out there to be myself. When I returned to the UK it all came flooding back and I started hating what I was seeing in the mirror – absolutely despising myself. I decided, "Right, so this is what I've got to do." And then I just started looking things up.'

The idea that the military, as an institution, has an irreparable culture of prejudice – and that this should be an argument for dismantling the entire thing – does nothing to help the actual victims of such prejudice. There's an assumption that this is a valid point of view because these problems are so well known that no one who's openly queer would set foot in this world anyway, but this ignores the varied reasons why people enter the forces in the first place.

In Christina's case, a major motive was that the military was perceived as masculine. She was struggling with her gender identity and hoped that by heading down this road she could hide who she really was, even to herself: but in the end this simply wasn't possible. The separation between civilian life and military life meant that for Christina, most of her interactions immediately after coming out were with other service people who were legally bound by the anti-discrimination rules of the British armed forces. Even if someone had a problem with her being trans, Christina told me, the RAF treats such incidents so seriously that they would never dare say anything transphobic for fear of losing their job and being prosecuted under laws unique to the forces. There's no point where it's ever 'easy' being a visibly trans person, but being supported from the very start of the process of transitioning can make an enormous difference in the long term. Rather than adding further pain to the issue as you might be inclined to imagine, coming out as trans in the RAF was, for Christina, significantly less traumatic than if she had done it in civilian life.

I specifically mentioned the current rules in the US, Britain and Israel to highlight how substantially different Christina's outcome could have been were she American. It's one thing for gender dysphoria to prevent someone entering the US military in the first place, but a whole other issue for someone already serving to come out as trans. Coming out may lead to an instant discharge, and often, for someone whose entire adult life has been spent in the military, it simply isn't an option – for financial *and* emotional reasons – to do something that'll get you fired. This doesn't mean there are no trans people serving in the US forces, it just means that trans people who do serve in the US forces are unable to come out and take the steps towards transitioning. The government's argument that gender dysphoria is a mental illness which prevents soldiers from doing their job properly doesn't hold up, as is proven by their more liberal allies who have allowed trans people to serve for some time. Even more infuriating is that studies have repeatedly shown improvements in the mental health and general well-being of trans people post-transition: is it any shock that someone who has hidden their true identity from the world their entire life and pretended to be something they're not becomes happier and more stable when they can finally live how they want, and openly be themselves? The ban on trans people in the US military doesn't stop trans people serving, it only stops them serving as their happiest, most mentally stable selves. And it gets worse.

Gender dysphoria is a complex condition, and a uniquely difficult thing with which trans people have to deal, but all too often it's discussed in a reductive way – including by those who are sympathetic to and supportive of trans issues – as being a wholly personal, individual crisis of identity. In fact, it could be argued that most, if not all, of the emotional anguish and pain associated with gender dysphoria is the fault of society and culture – i.e. everyone else. Because we have such rigid ideas of gender and encourage people from birth to follow a very specific path based on what genitals were observed in the delivery room, anyone who feels they don't fully align with this is essentially told they're just fucked up and backwards and wrong. For a lot of trans people it takes years just to accept and admit to themselves that they are who they are. Some, sadly, may not even come to this acceptance of themselves before they die. Trans people are usually aware, on some level, of their difference from early on in childhood, and for trans children lucky enough to grow up in progressive, accepting homes and societies, life can be a lot easier: by delaying the onset of puberty through hormone treatment, trans kids can put off potentially traumatic changes to their bodies long enough to satisfy doctors their gender dysphoria isn't 'just a phase' and transition before adulthood, something which has shown very promising results. However, most trans people don't have that option, and instead have to endure many more years of being forced to ignore what their brain tells them, and conform to their assigned gender. As was the case with Christina, this can lead to denial and over-compensation, and here's where the military enters into it all.

Christina went into the RAF partly *because* it was perceived as being masculine, at a time when she was in denial, still trying to present as male and eager to conceal her true identity from even herself. When, eventually, she felt unable to continue this way, she sought advice from her doctor, accepted to herself she was a woman and came out publicly via Facebook. She told me the night that she posted that update was the first time she had slept properly in years; finally able to drop her guard, her personality immediately softened too. I actually knew Christina (pre-transition) from school, although not closely, and in those days I considered her to be quite aggressive and unpleasantly macho, which is one of the reasons why we weren't really friends. When I first spoke to her after she came out, all of that had melted away, and it became clear it had just been for show. The overwhelming support her colleagues gave her confirmed what she had believed, that the RAF was the right place to come out, and every step of the way she was given the help and attitudes needed to begin her transition.

The existence of Christina's specific job – RAF police officer – hints at the insular nature of the armed forces: the RAF police keep order and enforce the law within their bases, both domestic and foreign, in the exact same way as police in civilian society. The military is a world of its own, to the extent that families of service people often live with them in their own little villages, and so everything – your culture, your social life – revolves around your work when you're serving in the military. It's understandable then, that for Christina, having the support of her colleagues meant everything.

Had she been in the United States, her life would have taken a very different path after leaving school for the military. Aside from the logistical aspect of potentially losing your job, such laws are also reflected in the culture of military personnel. If a particular group is officially excluded from service by those who make the rules, it's effectively telling everyone else in the military that it's okay to erase the existence and autonomy of said group altogether. Ban gay people from service, and you're sending the message that all gays are lesser humans and giving soldiers free licence to mock or disparage them. The same applies to trans people, and for those who have yet to come to terms with their identity on a personal level, such an environment will only push them further into denial. The result, for someone trying to pass as male, will be to overcompensate and push back with a particularly toxic display of hyper-masculinity.

Christina's specific situation is incredibly rare: trans people make up a small percentage of the total population and I would hazard a guess that they're also less likely proportionally to pursue a military career than cis people. You're probably asking why, then, I spent so long discussing this issue, but the answer is that it's just an extreme example of something I believe is worryingly widespread in this part of society. See, joining the military in order to boost one's image of masculinity may not be something a great deal of in-denial trans women are doing, but it's something a whole lot of men sure as hell are.

A Canadian friend of mine recently spoke of her shock after talking to a younger cousin during a family holiday and discovering the misinformed, violent motives behind his decision to enlist in the Royal Canadian Air Force. For understandable reasons, she doesn't want her cousin to be identified, so asked that his name be changed to Stephen.

'I asked Stephen why he wanted to be a pilot. He said "mostly I want to bomb all the Afghanis". I asked incredulously, "why?" He said, "for everything they've done". I raised my voice, "what have they done?" He raised his too and said, "you know, 9/11 and shit". He said he wanted to flatten their land and fuck them over, they don't deserve to live. I asked again, why this was his mission. He said he had seen some stuff. I guess he had gone to some training and they had shown him videos. He began calling me civilian and dismissing me, as if he had seen some great light and I was just a part of the machine.'

His remarks aren't entirely surprising, and echo the factually incorrect rhetoric heard across the United States about how Afghans and Iraqis are to blame for 9/11. In addition, as my friend pointed out to her cousin, Canada may border the US and share much of its world views, but it's not the same country and wasn't the intended target of the World Trade Center attacks.

'Two of my other cousins, who are the same age as Stephen boiled (this attitude) down to the culture of the suburb Stephen lives in: a suburb of a suburb, where boys are bored and destructive.'

An awful lot of what we associate with the military has seeped into civilian life. Nowhere in the world are servicemen and women treated so vocally with respect and admiration than in the United States; the country *adores* those who supposedly protect them. You know what else America has a unique obsession with? Guns. Civilian ownership of firearms has gone through the roof, and a lot of Americans take immense pride in their constitution's Second Amendment: the right to bear arms. The Second Amendment dates from colonial times and was originally intended to ensure that Americans could fight off British oppressors should the need arise. It essentially started life as an extension of the military, something which remains evident today. High capacity automatic weapons have little use in hunting or as a defence against home invaders, and yet a significant number of civilian Americans own them, these machines of war.

As I write this at the end of 2015, the US has already seen more mass shootings* than there have been days in the year.

* 'Mass shootings' is a tricky term to define and there are no agreed-upon definitions in law, but a number of sources including the FBI and Congressional Research Service suggest for something to qualify as a mass shooting there must be at least four victims (usually fatal) not including the shooter, and it must take place in a relatively short span of time and in a single location – distinguishing it from spree or serial killing.

What was once a shocking event has now become routine; reports of attacks are delivered and consumed as casually as the weather forecast. Most of the time it's an utterly senseless crime, but that doesn't stop the media speculating and trying to ascribe meaning: if the attacker was brown, it was terrorism; if young and white, a troubled 'lone wolf' with mental health issues. Maybe it was racially motivated, possibly religious or political, or simply a personal vendetta by a disgruntled former employee or ex-lover. It prompts calls for tighter gun control and better access to mental healthcare, but little ever changes, not least the constant need of the rolling news cycle to question *why* it happened. But in spite of all their speculation, there is little that links these mass shootings, except for one thing (and it's rarely acknowledged, even by those seeking to make sense of them): the vast, vast majority – around 98% – are committed by men.

If 98% of mass shootings in America were committed by Muslims, or black people, or fans of heavy metal, this fact would be on every newspaper's front page and talked about incessantly on every television channel. After the high school massacre in Columbine, the media drove itself into a frenzy trying to blame musicians like Marilyn Manson for the attack just because the perpetrators listened to his music – and that was a single incident. Similarly, violent video games have long been lambasted by campaigners for their supposed role, but given the fact women make up more than half of all gamers[22] you'd expect to see a few more of them gunning people down indiscriminately if this was the case.

Men do generally tend to be more violent than women and

are certainly more prone to reacting physically when feeling angry or threatened, but any argument that violence on this scale is caused by something biological doesn't stand up to scrutiny. While it may be in our instinct to fight in the heat of the moment, mass shootings are usually meticulously planned and thought through well in advance – and rarely seem to be the result of someone who happens to be fully armed getting pissed off as he goes about his daily business, and reacting there and then.

There's no single reason why America has more mass shootings than any other developed country. It goes without saying that its lax gun control laws are a major factor, and I don't doubt that its lack of universal healthcare prevents mentally ill people getting the treatment they would be able to elsewhere and that this, in turn, may be a contributor. However, there are countries with roughly comparable rates of firearm ownership which see proportionally far fewer mass shootings, and mental illness in perpetrators is a lot less common than some (namely people who oppose stricter gun control) would have you believe. It seems almost undeniable that mass shootings are largely a symptom of culture.

Consider the following points:

- Mass shootings in the US are often committed by people using high-capacity, automatic weapons, ownership of which is restricted in most other developed countries to the military. (By this logic, it's fair to say that America and American civilians are militarised in a way that no other western country is.)

- The military is an inherently masculine institution, the world over. Historically, only men could serve, and even in some countries that claim to have equal opportunities in their armed forces, women are still prevented from serving in certain frontline duties today.
- The overwhelming majority of mass shootings in America are committed by men.

I'm not asking you to blindly accept the theory that most mass shootings are a direct result of toxic masculinity, but do you at least see the link? In a media that's obsessed with trying to find meaning in such meaningless violence, does this not warrant consideration? America glorifies warfare to the extent that any adult who's not been caught for a crime can arm themselves as heavily as a soldier with relative ease.

It teaches that there are few things more noble than serving your country in battle and idolises guns as a symbol of power and freedom. But the honour and bravery with which war has long been associated is now so far detached from any semblance of reality, it's become quite contradictory and, in some respects, insulting to servicemen and women.

Picture that most American of all holidays, the 4th of July. In a modern context, Independence Day is just as much about saluting those who continue to defend the country's 'freedom' (both those currently serving in the military, as well as veterans) as the founding fathers themselves. How does America go about these celebrations? Big ol' explosions in the sky, or fireworks as they're better known. One of the problems with fireworks, as CNN noted[23] is:

Loud noises that sound like gunfire and other explosive blasts can trigger post-traumatic stress disorder. The US Department of Veteran Affairs estimates 11% to 20% of military members who have served in Iraq or Afghanistan suffer from the condition in a given year.

'I can't stand my country's constant hero worshipping,' Josh Huddleston says. 'I think it's a result of Vietnam. For people returning from Vietnam, we pretty much fucked them over. We didn't take care of them and mostly treated them like shit upon their return. Sometime after that, we realised that's not how people should be treated after going to war so we moved to the opposite extreme: every service member is a war hero. Which, of course, isn't true. I reached a point long ago where I'd go out of my way to avoid the subject of me having served, just so I wouldn't have to hear the person say "Thank you for your service!" I know it always comes from a positive place, I just don't want to hear it. The fact is there are all sorts of good and bad people who join up. They don't deserve praise by default. Many troops and veterans have a sense of entitlement, though, and expect it. Anyway, the hero-worship only makes more young boys want to join up, so they too can be "honoured" and appreciated. The last time our military really fought for our freedom was World War Two. Americans are collectively bullshitting themselves by thinking otherwise. This thought makes me feel very alone, because I know so few who would ever acknowledge it.'

Once upon a time, soldiers were admired and respected for protecting their country – keeping its citizens safe and upholding its beloved values and freedoms – and on the surface it would seem like these reasons hold true today. But dig a little deeper and more sinister motives appear. The anti-immigration rhetoric in America in 2015 was stunning: Donald Trump kept his place as front runner for the Republican presidential nomination despite calling for a ban on *all* Muslims entering the country, later saying family members of terrorists should be killed – the man who, at the time of writing, is currently the favourite to lead the Republicans in the 2016 general election literally advocated committing war crimes, to much applause. In such a bloodthirsty nation, it felt like soldiers were now being openly celebrated as killers by people with little preference for who exactly was being killed, as long as they were brown.

A remarkable poll in December 2015 showed that '30% of Republican primary voters nationally say they support bombing Agrabah'. Agrabah, if you don't know, is the fictional country in Aladdin. Writing in the *Guardian*, executive director of the Freedom of the Press Foundation Trevor Timm noted[24]:

> Republican voters, urged on by the Republican candidates, are now eager to bomb anywhere that has a Muslim-sounding name regardless of whether it comes from a cartoon. While the poll itself may be amusing, it's not exactly surprising given the cartoonish levels of tough-guy militarism that spews from the mouth of every Republican candidate as they try to one-up each other on who would start more wars harder and quicker.

This pro-bombing trend had been on a palpable increase ever since 9/11, as had the number of domestic mass shootings.

People weren't cheering on soldiers for protecting the lives of American civilians, they were cheering them on for slaughtering 'the enemy'. If the new spirit in American politics really was about protecting American lives, they would have instead called for stricter gun control: because, since 2001, far more Americans have died being shot by other Americans than have been killed in terrorist attacks.

Huddleston admits: '9/11 changed everything. Americans are terrified of everyone. Nothing is simple, but it's really that simple. It's had a dehumanising effect on how we perceive others – and each other – and I think it has led to a more sinister view of who we're killing.'

It could be argued quite easily that, ever since 9/11, American citizens have increasingly treated soldiers who kill large numbers of 'the enemy' with adulation, and seen them as idols of masculinity. But you don't have to be a soldier to do what soldiers are loved for doing, and in the US the soldier's tools necessary for such an act are within easy reach of almost every adult. One of the reasons why male suicide is such a prominent issue right now is the gender disparity, with three to four times as many men taking their own lives as women. Women are just as able to kill themselves as men, and are even more likely to suffer from mental illness, so the suicide rate has brought to light the way men are affected by societal notions of masculinity (with harmful results). In America, women have the same access to weapons as men, and again, are more likely to suffer from mental illness, so why are most mass shootings committed by men? You can dismiss my theory – that these shootings are largely to do with issues of masculinity – because it is just a theory, but you can't ignore the cold hard facts. If we can accept that toxic masculinity is a cause of suicide, then we must at least acknowledge that it's a factor in mass shootings.

In May 2014, Elliot Rodger killed six people in Isla Vista, California before taking his own life. Noah Berlatsky, writing in *The Atlantic*[25] commented on Rodger's 'poisonous ideals of masculinity' and the role they played in the spree:

> Rodger's horrifying violence, the videos he posted, and the way he saw himself are all extreme. But they're also a reflection of the way poisonous ideals of masculinity affect men. To some extent, I've felt the frustration Rodger felt, and I think other men may feel it as well. This is not an excuse for Rodger's actions, but something more painful: a confrontation of the ways in which he's not deviant, but typical. Acknowledging that seems like an important part of making sure this kind of thinking doesn't remain typical any longer.
>
> In his YouTube videos and a 137-page manifesto he wrote, Rodger's frustration toward women is constantly couched in terms of his hatred and envy of other men. "My problem is girls," he says, but adds, "I deserve girls much more than all those slobs." The threats in his final video are aimed at women, but they're also directed at men:
>
> "All you girls who rejected me and looked down upon me, and, you know, treated me like scum while you gave yourselves to other men. And all you men, for living a better life than me. All of you sexually-active men. I hate you. I hate all of you and I can't wait to give you exactly what you deserve. Utter annihilation."

I will go into more detail about the frustration of male virginity and sexuality in the later chapter 'Losing It', but for now I wanted to bring up Rodger's case as an example of the deadly, murderous side of masculinity – his crimes were motivated by a hatred of women for denying him sex, and of other men for being more sexually active than himself, which suggests that a fear of emasculation drove Rodger in a major way. This murderous behaviour is not surprising in the US: a highly militarised civilian society which today equates war-like violence with masculinity and heroism.

There's little doubt that for my dad's dad, war was the single biggest cause of his toxic behaviour. I've argued consistently throughout this book that the two world wars are responsible for the most harmful shift in what we perceive to be masculine behaviour, so it may seem unlikely (or at the very least highly contradictory) that I have any words or praise for the military – but I do. For Rex, my maternal grandfather, his experience in the forces was very different indeed – due to his asthma he never saw active service during the war, but nevertheless spent several years in the RAF, loading bombs onto the planes before they flew out. After reading my interview with Christina, my mum told me that the support Christina had been given by the air force reminded her of how important the RAF was to her father. Rex had seemingly had an unhappy start in life and was made to feel by his family like he didn't belong – his father, in particular, was disappointed that Rex was interested in 'feminine' activities such as gardening, and was not the sport-loving 'lad's lad' he wanted him to be. It wasn't until he joined the RAF that Rex was truly taken care of – they looked after him, fed him well, treated his asthma and gave him a sense of purpose and belonging. For the first time in his life, he actually felt loved. Similarly, Josh Huddleston agrees that, on a personal level, the military changed him in an overall positive way.

'It got me out of an isolated, rural part of the country and let me see other, different peoples. A life-changing moment for me was when I deployed to Djibouti and went into Djibouti City for the first time. It really gave me an appreciation for having been fortunate enough to come into existence in a country that has everything from clean drinking water and a steady food supply to transportation, electricity, and other luxuries I'd taken for granted my whole life. When a kid (probably 8–10 years old) followed me around for a while in Djibouti City and eventually found an opportunity to take my half-full bottle of water from my hand and guzzle it down and then run off, it had an effect on me. These kinds of specific experiences are probably good for Americans who join up and get to go abroad.

'It changed me politically for the better, I'd argue. It made me more self-aware and confident while also humbling me. It let me let go of God and religion. It eventually made me *comfortable* with my masculinity, not feeling the need to be "tough", or present myself as such. It opened my mind to not only listening to shitty, aggressive nu-metal bands. Maybe all of that was the result of being in for a couple of years and wanting to get the fuck out, knowing I still had a few years left. I met so many interesting people from different parts of the country and world. And the shared hardships forged what will almost certainly be the best friendships I'll ever have. Having been out for almost nine years now, I've made numerous new friends in my post-Corps life, but sadly, not like the friends I made while I was in. Why does sharing in misery do this sort of thing? I've no idea. It also got me a high security clearance and allowed me to transition to a good IT job when I got out. In the end, it was good for me, despite the occasional survivor's guilt I have, having known people who didn't make it.'

Like masculinity itself, institutions such as the military can't be discussed in black and white. I don't deny the horrors for which they're responsible and have no problem seeing why plenty of people write them off entirely. Especially in the wake of the War on Terror campaigns in Afghanistan and Iraq, from which evidence of torture and gruesome treatment by western forces has emerged, it can be easy to view the military as evil – and why would you ever want to support such a system? As an ideology, this way of thinking is fine, but in practice it just makes things worse. As a pacifist you may view the military as fundamentally irreparable and believe that those who choose to join the armed forces do so knowing what to expect and are therefore responsible for anything that happens to them – be it injury, death or poor treatment at the hands of their own people – as a result. I am certainly guilty of this as far as my views of the police goes: when honest, good officers complain that they are not trusted or are unfairly abused by the public, I have little sympathy for them because I consider the institution itself corrupt and dangerous – and by making that choice to become police, they willingly choose to be representatives of this institution and all of its flaws. The same applies to politics: we may have been served well by an MP for many years, but if we're angry or disappointed in the actions of their party, then it's often this that sways our vote instead of the individual.

Humans can be stubborn and so tied to our principles that we refuse to accept a compromise, even if it's objectively the best outcome we could hope for. I know that we're not just going to decide one day to scrap all the police, of course I know that. I wouldn't be surprised if hostility towards decent officers could in turn make them more likely to start treating people badly, or simply drive them out of the force – and if that's the case, then by holding on to my extreme views, I'm making matters worse. It's not my fault if they react this way, but opinions like mine might still have an impact.

This is why it's important that, whatever we think about the military as an institution, we have to be prepared to put this aside if we genuinely want things to improve. Consider the following:

1) There is arguably no career more closely linked to perceptions of masculinity than the military
2) The single biggest employer in the world is the US Department of Defense, and armed forces in most countries are generally one of the largest employers

You can probably see where I'm going with this.

There are a lot of reasons why people decide to join the military, good and bad. In many countries it's still considered the most noble and patriotic profession you could choose, and while you might disagree with that assertion, there's no shortage of recruits whose intentions, at least to begin with, were admirable. I don't doubt for a second though that the way it's perceived as a masculine pursuit influences a significant number of young men.

Christina's circumstances were extraordinary, I'll admit, but her reasons for joining the armed forces are indicative of something much bigger: a culture that purports to be the solution to an individual's insecurities about their masculinity.

Becoming a soldier won't make you any more of a man, but those who think it will are arguably the most at risk of falling victim to other toxic ideas of masculinity. And though there are clearly some happy endings, the reality is that until this issue is addressed, masculinity in the military is going to continue to wreak havoc. In spite of his own experience, Josh Huddleston tells me the usual story is not so positive.

'For others, I think it can only reinforce already-bad behaviour and characteristics. I see a lot of people get out and they become even more obsessed with macho shit and "toughness". The sad thing is they don't realise it. For my generation *as a whole*, overall I'd say being in the military has probably been more bad than good, and that's solely because of the wars we've fought. 9/11 really did change the US. It made us afraid, and willing to allow the Bush administration to get us into Iraq, which destroyed countless lives on both sides – not to mention the increased instability we now have all over the Middle East. It was a great betrayal, for me anyway. Among the three friends I graduated high school with and went through boot camp with, one of them died in Iraq. Another was almost killed in Iraq after being hit with an RPG – he was flown to Germany, operated on multiple times, and then sent directly back to his unit in Iraq;

he earned a second Purple Heart after being charged by a bull that was being grazed by gunfire. I'm not kidding. But I digress. Perhaps this doesn't really speak to the subject of masculinity and the military, but whatever factors lead to men and women joining – which, I'd argue is an obsession with masculinity – this has been the result.'

It's clear that there's still much progress needed in this world, but unfortunately a lot stands in its way. To make matters more complicated, there are barriers presented by both ends of the political spectrum. Of course, the old, conservative, hard-right types tend to oppose any sort of social progression particularly in their beloved military.

As support for LGBT rights has grown, events like Pride have entered into mainstream acceptance, something which has caused a lot of controversy within campaign groups. Corporate sponsorship of Pride from banks like Barclays has come under fire (in the case of Barclays, because of the company's history of human rights violations), and similar criticisms have been aimed at the inclusion of floats representing the armed forces, the police, and the Conservative Party – all of which have at some point been responsible for oppression of the gay community. Left-leaning LGBT people feel it's insulting to allow such groups to take part in Pride because of their past actions, and believe it allows them to evade responsibility and erase public knowledge of such wrongdoing. However, others think it's necessary to allow these institutions to move on from their past in order to increase the visibility of support and make progress.

A couple of weeks after I interviewed Christina, she invited me to join her at Pride in London, which she attended in full

uniform. When I asked how she felt about Barclays' involve-
ment, I was surprised to hear that she, as a trans woman, was
far less cynical about it than me, but later realised how much
sense her stance made. She had joined the RAF while she was
still presenting as a cis man, driven by the hope that the masculine environment would put an end to her struggle with identity.
When it became clear this wasn't going to happen, the support
of the RAF and its commitment to the LGBT cause was vital in
allowing her to be who she really was.

Like I said earlier, Christina's reasons for entering the military – ie to reinforce her masculinity – were an extraordinary
example of a very ordinary culture. As long as the military is
perceived as being a masculine institution, it will attract some of
those most at risk of perpetuating the behaviours we would generally refer to as toxic masculinity. If soldiers are received into
an institution that bans women or LGBT people from serving,
their entire environment will be reflective of this in a particularly
harmful way: not only will their attitudes towards these groups
be shaped by official doctrine from the highest level, automati-
cally rendering all other people as inferior to straight males, but
it will also severely limit their exposure to these groups in daily
life and prevent them from getting a most basic understanding
of anyone different to them. A more sensitive attitude towards
such groups would have a beneficial effect not only on the military, but also on society's view of masculinity as a whole.

In the UK, recruitment campaigns for the armed forces have
used as a selling point the wide array of non-combat related

training and education available to those who sign up: from driving lessons to cookery classes. One of the major problems for service people in the past was that when they eventually left the military for good, they struggled to find work because they lacked basic real world skills – they were, in many respects, like prisoners just released after decades locked up and unable to assimilate with society. Not wanting potential new recruits to be perturbed by this, the forces began to emphasise that you could make the necessary preparations for whatever career you could possibly want after leaving the military, and all on their dime, as you continued to earn your wages. Like I said earlier, military life is its own little world, and over time, awareness has grown of the necessary responsibilities to those who serve.

What we need to see now is a social commitment: to educate everyone in the forces not just in visible, employable trades, but emotionally too. Young men need to be taught how their masculinity can be defined in healthy, pro-active ways: that expressing their emotions needn't be avoided, that they can treat women decently and still be attractive to them. Most of all, they need to hear this from their peers and their superiors, the strong men they may not like but definitely respect, because these are the people they will actually listen to. The military has a duty to ensure, both for its own kind and the rest of society, that when these young men re-enter civilian life they are genuinely the positive male role models they're so often held up to be. Plenty of my peers I'm sure would outright reject the notion that soldiers could ever be something boys ought to be encouraged to look up to, but once more I believe that this is inevitable and thus requires a pragmatic approach if anything is to improve.

There's no chance we're going to see the link between masculinity and military disappear anytime soon, so now we have to focus our efforts on making this link as positive as we possibly can. Of course, such is the purpose of the military we cannot avoid certain attitudes reflective of masculinity pervading – soldiers are to some extent programmed to be killing machines. But if the military is going to be churning out people who are taken to be role models, they have a responsibility to examine exactly what sort of qualities they would like an ex-soldier to have. What we absolutely must avoid is a blind celebration of these men in uniform and a glorification of the weapons they hold, because this issue of the military reaches far beyond the institution itself.

The Ideal Man: Body Image, Consumerism and the Superficial Face of Modern Masculinity

The term 'metrosexual' was most likely coined in 1994 by the *Independent* journalist Mark Simpson, giving us a new word to discuss one of the most debated aspects of modern masculinity. There's no doubting the role played by physical appearance in how we perceive ourselves and others, and in many cases our first impressions of a person are based solely on how they dress and present themselves – after all, it takes only a split second to look at someone, while it might take minutes or even hours to make a judgment of their personality based on conversation and behaviour. Even those who totally oppose the idea that we should be defined by fashion know better than to turn up to a job interview in scruffy, unironed clothes, sporting unkempt hair; your talent and intelligence count for nothing if you've not bothered to make any effort with how you look. When it comes to looks men may not be held to anywhere near the same expectations as women (something for which I am grateful as I write this in a dubious t-shirt/

boxers combo), but they can still make all the difference when it comes to how others think of us.

When we talk about other, non-aesthetic areas of masculinity, there seems to be a fairly strong consensus of what a man should and shouldn't be. Ideas that are rooted in a more philosophical context – courage, for example – are pretty much universally accepted as being desirable traits of the male gender, and although what we consider to be courageous may vary from person to person, male bravery, by and large, is synonymous with masculinity. Just as we may have different ideas of what constitutes weakness or strength, we, as a society, are fully in agreement that strength is something men should possess in order to be viewed as masculine.

Physical appearance, however, is unique in this respect. We all have our own beliefs regarding what the perfect man should look like, and this is generally linked to sexual preference: some people might idealise the suited-up and slickly groomed Don Draper image; others may think a man's at his finest sweating into sportswear; others yet prefer the skinny, scruffy rock star vibes. Of course, this subjectivity is no different to how we disagree on the definition of courage, but looks aren't quite as black and white.

There's a whole other school of thought that takes into consideration the impact a man's appearance has on his masculinity, but rather than concerning what he *does* about it, it focuses on how much he *cares* about it. In this mindset, the thing that's applauded above all else for its expression of masculinity is a total sense of apathy.

Something I will explore in further detail later on in the book is the relationship between masculinity and sexuality, but, while I'll try to keep this short, it's worth dipping into for just a second here. The reason 'metrosexual' is, to my mind, at least, such a culturally significant word, is that it is used to describe something that has no real relationship with sexuality (someone's sexual orientation or preference) and is rather all about money, class and fashion. The 'sexual' may refer in part to a metrosexual man's desire to be physically attractive, but more than that, it's a reminder of a persistent trope: a man who cares about his appearance any more than is deemed normal is probably not straight. We all know men who scoff at fashion, and it's quite possible you personally do so, I certainly did in the past. Even those who believe style is important may adhere to a fixed idea of what style is, and criticise the faddish nature of fashion and anyone who partakes. A lot of us think less of these men (the generation who fought in the war wouldn't have worn such stupid apparel!) and some of fashion's biggest critics quite openly believe that an interest in personal appearance is indicative of effeminate or homosexual behaviour.

Really, it's all the fault of capitalism

Like most modern words, 'metrosexual' was born out of cultural change, necessitated by a discussion that hadn't previously existed. It signalled increasing focus on more superficial aspects of masculinity, and arguably evolved from the consumerism that began in the 1980s, originally in Ronald Reagan's America and then spreading across the Atlantic. The era's male pop culture anti-heroes such as *American Psycho*'s Patrick Bateman and

Fight Club's Tyler Durden were obsessed, in one way or another, with excess. These fictional studies of men, and the way in which capitalism defined their masculinity, were a direct response to contemporary society. Whatever your opinion of such characters or their creators, the mere fact that they exist reveals how masculinity evolved and brought new challenges towards the end of the 21st century, and the effect this has had on younger generations of men.

Around this time, we saw the emergence of a new kind of man, one who was termed by the ever-inventive media 'the New Man'. For some people, the New Man was defined by his dismissal of traditional gender roles, getting his hands dirty with housework and looking after his kids. For others, it was more of a fashion and style thing, their idea of the New Man fitting snugly within the definition of 'metrosexual'. Either way, it was a time of soft revolution for the gender, and capitalism was beginning to cotton on. I already touched upon this in my earlier essay 'The Dawn of Man', but will give a brief recap for the purposes of this chapter.

In Britain, the 1980s were the nail in the coffin for the country's working class. Mass closures hit the mining industry hard, and during this period much of the country's factory work began to be outsourced, decimating jobs that were primarily held by men. Privatisation of public services meant that their primary concern was now to ensure maximum profit for their shareholders, and this was often done to the detriment of their workforce. The first moves were made towards deregulating banks, and the general focus of the economy began to shift away from manufacturing and towards financial services. While high unemployment left a previously comfortable working class struggling to survive, those on the other end of the spectrum were able to earn more than ever before, creating an enormous wealth gap between society's richest and poorest. This, obviously, affected everyone in the country – but for men it may have been responsible for the most widespread change in attitudes since World War Two.

The pride of the British working class in the mid-20th century is well-documented. Post-war, the establishment of the NHS and the welfare state heralded the beginning of a fairer country, one that would strive to help all of its citizens regardless of their wealth, and support the workers who would literally rebuild the nation. Generations of families thrived in this way until the decline of industry, and when that happened, working class men, knowing nothing else, were left feeling utterly worthless. The psychological and economic devastation this caused is still apparent in some mining towns, where even those born after the closures are plagued by unemployment and the poor mental health associated with decades of despair.

At the same time as this was happening, the middle class (or, at least, the upper-middle class) was thriving, and jobs that had always commanded a respectable salary, such as those in banking, were now paying previously unimaginable amounts. Unsurprisingly, the working class today has all but disappeared, as younger generations have had little choice but to pursue service-based work or face a life of unemployment. Most of the industry jobs like mining had been done by men, mainly because of their physical capabilities, and previously this may have been all a man required to feel comfortable in his masculinity. He was needed, by both his work and his family, almost entirely because he was a man. When these jobs died out, our idea of masculinity changed for good, and became something altogether more superficial.

I won't bore you by repeating the points I made earlier in the book about the importance of work for men and masculinity, but the financial independence women were starting to achieve meant that they had more autonomy over everything, and their decisions no longer had to be influenced entirely by someone else's money. For men, whose suitability as partners may once have been judged solely by their ability to provide financially, this presented a new barrier to finding a wife. Historically, emphasis was placed on a woman's looks because the only way she could survive financially was if she was provided for by a husband; her only purpose was to serve and please a man, and if she wasn't attractive enough, she would never marry. She couldn't really afford to be picky, she just had to find a husband capable of providing for her: which meant men didn't really have to worry about their looks as long as they had cash. That all changed when women entered the workplace: now they could more easily choose to be with someone they actually fancied. Imagine that, eh?

Men's fashion and style had of course existed long before this, but for the first time they had greater cause to worry about their appearance on a personal level. Mostly, though, as long as they combed their hair and owned at least one suit, men could get by just fine. And they did this! When we look at photos from the 40s and 50s taken in busy public places we're often blown away by how well dressed everyone is: all the men – regardless of class – wearing suits, the only indicator of their status being the style of hat they wore. Unlike in previous centuries when wealth was divided very unevenly, and clothes were a clear indicator of class (quite literally the difference of rags and fine robes), men's style was almost homogeneous, transcending any sense of class or wealth.

If we return again to the 80s, while the working class fell apart, men elsewhere in society were experiencing a level of wealth previously only enjoyed by aristocrats. With extraordinary disposable incomes, there was a new market for luxury goods: clothes, cars, electronics – anything that would give the buyer a chance to flash his cash. The same was true for less affluent, but still comfortable, middle-class folk; glitzy ad campaigns helped turn fashion into a branded commodity, people were told that they *needed* items they'd never previously thought about, and it all happened on a global scale that had never been seen before. Functionality or quality of items were ditched in favour of the logo they carried, and I'm sure many children remember the fear of going to school with the wrong stripes on their trainers.

Oh, like anyone has abs *that* defined

What better way to advertise such clothes than to have them worn by an impossibly handsome model or successful sports star? What better way to convince society that there is only one acceptable type of body women will find attractive; that masculinity is all about how you look. And there are no awkward, semi-weedy guys beaming out of the ad as they wear that t-shirt; no chubby blokes surrounded by beautiful women because he wears Lynx deodorant. That's not sexy, that wouldn't sell; only the most toned or most skinny, most tanned or most pale, tall men with perfectly coiffed hair can do that. It's everywhere, boys grow up surrounded by images like this, and no matter what anyone says to the contrary, they can't help but see the message: this is what a man should look like. Of course, the same is true for girls – and they have been exposed to it for much longer, and, arguably, with more intensity than boys. It's quite possibly because of this that measures have been taken to tackle body image issues in girls in recent years, while the effects on boys have been less well studied.

Regardless of gender, if a child is told repeatedly that beauty is defined by a single set of strict rules, and that this beauty is directly linked to success and happiness, they're probably going to believe it's true. As they become more aware of their own body – particularly after puberty sets in – every little characteristic that differs from what they've been told is attractive is perceived as a flaw, and something to be ashamed of or embarrassed about. Depending on their current mental state as well as environmental factors (stability of family, friendship group, relationships etc) they may be able to accept their body, and even grow to love it – but for some, the outcome can be much worse. It's widely accepted that the unrealistic standards of beauty we're exposed to in the media can contribute to psychological disorders related to body image. At a low level this can cause problems with self-esteem, anxiety and depression; more seriously, it can lead to potentially life-threatening eating disorders.

Male eating disorders have been on the rise in the last couple of decades, with the number of diagnoses up 27% since 2000[26]. Because eating disorders in boys and men haven't appeared on a large scale until much more recently than those in girls and women, diagnosis and treatment can be affected by problems unique to males. Indeed, due to the fact that eating disorders are so closely associated with women, male sufferers can be too embarrassed to seek help: as they feel that admitting to this may be emasculating. Efforts have been made to destigmatise eating disorders in women, but for men the subject is still considered taboo in many circles – and as with all mental illnesses, there can be a tendency to view it as a weakness, or even erase its existence completely. In an attempt to understand just how pervasive the social issues affecting male eating disorders are, I had a chat with journalist Huw Oliver, who suffered from anorexia in his teens.

'Just yesterday I spoke to an editor at a French magazine about some of the writing work I'd previously done and mentioned how I'd written about male anorexia. His response? "That exists...?" People simply don't know because the media doesn't speak about it – and the situation's much worse in France, it seems. Because the general public is uninformed, they're also less likely to be sympathetic and that makes those with eating disorders much less likely to speak up: so it's a vicious circle.'

Huw's illness first appeared around the age of 13, at a time when, he says, he 'had this idea of the ideal skinny man in my head, a kind of mythical figure who regularly fits into Topman 28-inch jeans and looks a bit like Julian Casablancas*. That's who I wanted to be, but how I got to the point where I started

* Frontman of garage rock band The Strokes, and very much a poster boy of the early 00s indie scene.

starving myself to get like that, I don't know. There was an undercurrent of depression, I think, as I didn't really have a great time at school, and anorexia I reckon became a way of channelling that into something I considered at the time to be productive and self-improving – making myself look better. I also would have had no clue at the time what depression and anxiety were, so perhaps making myself anorexic became a way of making my problem appear more understandable and more concrete in my head.'

'I do think media portrayals played into it as well. Not so much the hunky imagery we see in tabloids and glossies (and hence why over-exercising never came into the equation) but model-like skinniness and the slender indie look you might glean from the pages of *NME*. I think I did feel some level of attraction to these kind of figures and, going to a single-sex school, I was also surrounded by near-naked boy bodies in changing rooms etc every week. That didn't help – that just compounded the issue and made me aspire to own a body more like theirs, and more like these figures I saw in the media. Apart from that, like I say, feeling a little disillusioned and depressed generally was almost definitely the starting-point, and not being able to artic-ulate what was wrong, and god forbid that I tell anyone about it, my anorexia grew from there. It was reinforced, I'm sure, by these images I saw and by those surrounding me, plus also the general language we read in rubbishy magazines. I remem-ber seeing a copy of *Heat* from the time effectively endorsing a one-meal-a-day diet plan that Lily Allen was following, and looking back now, I'm pretty sure that inspired me on some subconscious level to do similar.'

I asked Huw in what ways he felt his gender and sense of masculinity exacerbated his condition and prevented him from seeking help. 'I would never have gone to speak to anyone about any small emotional problem I had, let alone confront my close family and friends with the details of mysterious private issues. Too embarrassing, and I thought it was no one's business. I was embarrassed by my body, embarrassed by the fact I was doing something to change it, and shy and afraid to talk about most things except music and assessments anyway. So I guess that therein lies that typical male tendency to shut oneself up and avoid emotional talk at all costs. None of my friends would have talked to me about similar such things, so why would I? Even once I'd started to eat more normally, I never fessed up to anyone, not even my parents, and I still find it very awkward talking about it today.

'Another thing is that how was I to know that what I was doing was anorexia? I wasn't – ostensibly – direly ill or in hospital, so it didn't feel like an illness. For me it was just a habit or hobby, something I did to make me look better, like going for a run or not eating dessert – but more extreme. And in any case, how could I have anorexia? It's for girls. I didn't have any girls who were friends, but I knew that anorexia was their preserve. When you hear about it in the news it always goes along with stats about the number of girls who get affected by eating disorders and there's rarely any mention of the male stats – which are lower, sure, but much higher than you might presume. There's more and more recognition of "bigorexia" and that kind of thing now, but male anorexia remains relatively unheard of. So there's that – I didn't think I could be anorexic because no one ever says "anyone can be affected". It's always "20% of schoolgirls suffer from eating disorders", end of story.

'I was only self-diagnosed and I wasn't open at all; I didn't talk about it until I was 20. And yes, I think much of that is down to our gendering of eating disorders as a mostly female phenomenon, and especially anorexia. For a boy, especially at a single-sex school in which "gay" and "pussy" are the routine insults, to suffer from such a feminine, unmanly problem would be the ultimate embarrassment. More broadly, I think it was down to a general reluctance to open up and talk about my issues, combined with this underlying sense of embarrassment. That's certainly what stopped me discussing it with friends and family, both at the time and afterwards, when I just acted like it never happened. At sixth form, I convinced myself my newfound skinniness was just my natural body shape, and others thought the same.'

Dadbods, and how the media portrays male beauty

There have certainly been attempts to diversify women's body types in media, with plus-size models finding themselves increasingly in demand. By displaying different types of bodies, young women are more likely to find themselves represented in a positive light and grow up believing that beauty is not defined as strictly as they've previously been told. However, there has yet to be any indication that the same steps are being taken with men: there are no plus size male models, and there is no major discussion of these issues in the media, and although the briefly popular 'dadbod' was used as a mostly complimentary term, its very name stood as a reminder that a less-than-impressive physique is only considered acceptable in older men.

When the actor Chris Pratt revealed his dramatic weight loss and newfound six pack, it was headline news, and he was celebrated left, right and centre for his newly-developed sexiness. His face hadn't changed, and he was no more charismatic than before, but suddenly he was being portrayed as a Hollywood hunk – all it told us was that there is only one male body type it's socially acceptable to find attractive. Female celebrity weight loss (or gain) continues to fill out the pages of trashy gossip mags, but few respectable, mainstream media outlets would go near this any more. Pratt, on the other hand, they lapped up with glee. The media objectification of women has, rightfully, been falling out of favour for some time, but at the same time almost seems to be rising for men. Listicles such as '12 hottest male teachers' have made their way onto huge websites like Buzzfeed, and inevitably, there is at least one comment below each pointing out how offended people would be if it was women instead of men. Male objectification of women is something that carries innumerable problematic issues, and due to its long history of entrenched sexism and misogyny, it's entirely different to women 'objectifying' men, which tends to mean quite simply 'enjoying their appearance' and not 'equating their looks to their worth as humans and perpetuating a dangerous entitlement to their bodies' – so yes, it's not quite the same thing. In that sense, 'objectifying men' is a bit like 'anti-white racism' (when while people believe they have been the victims of racism, they are ignoring the much deeper, historical implications of racism against, say, black people) and while it certainly exists, it does so on a completely different level and all too often serves to derail from the more pressing issues – in this case the objectification of women. That said, I believe such articles are a problem if they lack diversity – if all 22 of your '22 hottest men in their underwear, carrying dachshunds' are muscular and toned, then however light-hearted your intentions were, you are contributing to the same, fixed idea of how a man should look that boys have drilled into them their entire lives.

It's not just those with unconventionally attractive bodies who are hurt by this either, others are similarly shamed for being attracted to these people: think about phrases such as 'chubby chaser', used overwhelmingly as a pejorative to mock someone who's into larger people – and though it has its ety-mological roots within the gay community, it is generally used among heterosexuals in the context of women. It's all so bizarre and pointless when you think about it, because, fuck, beauty is entirely subjective. I've observed, on multiple occasions, large groups of men joking about 'fat girls', every last one of them agreeing that overweight women are objectively unattractive and that to sleep with one would be shameful and embarrassing, or 'a last resort'. They are just agreeing with what (western) society says, but it reminds me of how there are no openly gay pro-fessional footballers, and the statistical improbability of every player being straight – and what this tells us both about atti-tudes within the game and our human fear of not conforming.

In my experience, this is a bigger problem for men than for women. Women tend to be more open and willing to stray from social norms, particularly in issues regarding sex and rela-tionships. Women who consider themselves 'mostly straight' are more likely to have had same sex encounters than men, and are more likely in general to be bisexual. Researchers at the University of Notre Dame found that: 'While the majority of men are convinced they are either "100 per cent" homosexual or heterosexual, women have a much more fluid approach to relationships, based on who they meet'[27]. It's more than possible one of the reasons for this is that men feel the need for defined labels and fear that any experimentation would change their fundamental personality and harm their masculinity. You don't hear about women being concerned about being less feminine in the way you do about men and masculinity.

The rise of 'bigorexia' and unattainable body image

Portmanteaus like 'manorexia' and 'bigorexia' are words Huw Oliver hates – 'there's nothing funny about a man loathing his own body' – and I'm inclined to agree, but their rise in popularity echoes the rise of the trends they describe, even if they do serve to trivialise the matter. 'Bigorexia' refers to the unhealthy behaviour of some people – especially men – pushing themselves too far to attain a muscular, well-built physique. They may not be starving themselves in the way people with anorexia do, though their problems are no less real. You've probably noticed protein drinks becoming a much more familiar sight in the last half a decade or so, with global sales in the protein industry doubling between 2007 and 2012 and estimated to amount to £8 billion by 2017[28]. Originally targeted at bodybuilders and extreme fitness fanatics, the makers of protein shakes and other protein supplement products have started to reach out to ordinary people with claims of health-giving properties. The BBC noted[29] however, that:

>...there's an elephant in the room. People in the West usually already get more than enough protein.
>
>Healthy protein intake depends on weight, with a recommended intake figure of 0.8g per kg of weight per day often cited. Age is also a factor. Over the course of a day, the average man should be eating around 55g of protein, while a woman needs 45g, says the British Dietetic Association. In the US, the national public health body, the Centers for Disease Control and Prevention, recommends 56g for an average man and 45g for a woman.
>
>In the UK the mean intake for men is 86.5g per day, with women consuming 65g, says nutritionist Dr Helen Crawley. The CDC says "most adults in the United States get more than enough protein to meet their needs".

It seems we all get sucked in quite easily by these kinds of products, regardless of gender. Protein shakes are just one example of the many ways we're coerced by advertising and left susceptible to quick fixes and shortcuts if it concerns our bodies, but they're a particularly unique one – in that while many supplements claim to promote weight loss and thinness, protein is geared towards the opposite: bulking up. For men, they offer a solution to what society deems an unmasculine figure, one lacking size and brawn. 'Offer a solution' is a bit generous though – 'prey on our insecurities' may actually be more appropriate in this context.

I recently went to a small gym not far from where I live in Toronto and spoke to Ryan Atkins, a personal trainer there. He explained that one of the problems he consistently sees is young men not realising that there are fundamental differences in body types and trying to force themselves to change in a way that simply isn't possible. I was a little surprised to discover I apparently have 'a gymnast's body' (try telling that to my flabby, post-Christmas torso) and could bulk up quite easily if I so desired, whereas other men would be unable to achieve such size due to their frames. Atkins told me that a lot of men who go to commercial gyms have an idealised image in their head of what a man should look like even though that may not be a feasible shape for their own bodies, and are often reluctant to ask for help or advice, instead choosing to mimic other guys' workout routines. This can cause injury and, inevitably, disappointment when they don't wind up looking the way they wanted to. The rise of protein shakes shows how badly we want to conform with societal standards of beauty, despite that image often being unattainable.

We can't all be above average

When you stop and think about it, you realise that the number of people who do fit this template is a tiny fraction of the whole population. I mean, just look at how high rates of obesity are, and how not a single one of those people could be deemed sexy by our society's fairly narrow agreeable standards. And while you can dress a certain way and work out, you can't change the type of body you were born with or your looks (unless you can afford plastic surgery, which most of us can't). One of the most difficult – and ironic – issues facing men, is that in spite of the psychological harm we inflict on ourselves in striving to attain 'masculinity', when we believe we have failed in this mission, it can be even more damaging to our mental health. Men can be at their most dangerous – to others and themselves – when they feel their masculinity has been challenged (something I will return to later). So while our behaviour can itself be unhealthy in the long term, if we are able to convince ourselves that it is nonetheless masculine, it might be enough to avert a crisis in the short term. For this very reason, the way in which physical appearance is equated with masculinity is terrifying. As far as personalities go, we can act masculine to ourselves and others, but we can't change our bodies or looks. We can't make ourselves taller or broader or more handsome; these attributes come down to the luck of the draw, genetic good fortune. Unrealistic beauty standards are harmful to everyone, but for modern men, the way they're linked to our masculinity – and the fragility of this – means they're especially dangerous.

When a man feels insecure about his physical appearance and believes others may consider him less masculine as a result, he may try to compensate for this in other areas. Unfortunately, as I've explored throughout the book, common misunderstandings as to what masculinity is can mean it manifests itself in negative forms, such as increased aggression or risky behaviour. Most toxic masculinity is a result of some sort of insecurity or fear of how others perceive you; it's why it's so predominantly a cis-het issue. Gay men are every bit as capable of being traditionally masculine, but are less likely to exhibit such toxic behaviour because they don't feel the need to prove themselves, or follow a straight man's narrative of their gender. The fact that much of this behaviour is motivated by a fear of being perceived as effeminate or gay is telling, and men who are comfortable in their sexuality and gender are much less likely to behave in such an extreme way.

Could porn be our saviour?

There is a light at the end of the tunnel: attitudes are changing on the fringes of society, and as these voices continue to grow stronger, the mainstream will begin to reflect this – acceptance of plus-size models and representation of more diverse women's bodies exemplify how broader definitions of beauty have soared in popularity over the last couple of years, and it's likely that the way we talk about men's bodies will follow suit. The internet has played a big part in this, and is almost certainly responsible for sociological progression occurring faster than at any point in history, but hope for the future may lie in the web's least likely place: porn. If you're tempted to stop reading at this point, you should know that the irony of such a statement in this very chapter is not lost on me. As I will explore later on in the book, porn is not without its problems, and Christ knows professional porn stars in airbrushed, 'glamorous' productions are directly responsible for the insecurities of many young people – in this respect, it's just as detrimental, if not more so, than any other factor. However, this is only one 'genre', if you will.

Back in the days before the internet, a porn consumer's only options were top-shelf magazines or the mysterious back room in video rental shops, so the content itself was extremely limited, and thus followed a pretty rigid idea of what those in the business thought would sell. That is to say, it wouldn't be worth producing something that focused on a niche kink because very few people would buy it. But when the internet took off, it revolutionised the way porn was consumed and distributed: you could reach a massive global audience without the costs of physical media and cater to more diverse tastes. Even more significant was the speed at which mass-produced, inexpensive video recording technology appeared, to the point where the majority of young people in western countries today carry in their pockets a device capable of capturing high-definition footage at a moment's notice. Anyone who wanted to could now create their own amateur pornography and upload it for the whole world to see – and boy, did they.

The availability and, above all, the variety of porn today is quite frankly *phenomenal*. 'Rule 34' is a fairly well known joke amongst people who've been online for a few years, stating: if it exists, there's porn of it – and the reality probably isn't too far off this. Critics say this normalises behaviour they perceive to be 'abnormal', and I am inclined to agree, but unlike them I don't believe 'abnormal' is synonymous with 'bad', as long as all parties involved are consenting adults. Porn, by its very definition, serves to titillate and arouse the consumer and does so successfully because he or she is, in essence, attracted to what they see. If you look at the categories on any porn site, it's clear that what men (and women, who are increasingly partaking) are attracted to is completely different to what society suggests. Statistics from sites that make them publicly available show us that some of the most popular categories are those we're often shamed for admitting we like, and in the long term this may prove to be beneficial to us all.

Porn is ubiquitous amongst young men, to the point where researchers wanting to interview those who'd never viewed porn were unable to find any. Internet porn is private and non-judgmental – when you click on something niche, you don't get a pop-up mocking you for your kinks – and though we may not be comfortable admitting what we like to our friends, that it exists in abundance online can help us accept we're not weird or alone. Being comfortable in our own thoughts is the first step towards us feeling confident enough to speak out – and when we get to that point, we might well realise that the same is true of our friends.

Call me idealistic and misguided (everyone else does) but I believe that if we are able to accept there is no shame in finding unconventionally attractive people sexy, we may also find it easier to come to terms with the insecurities about our own bodies and, by doing so, tackle the harmful link between physical attributes and masculinity. There is very little we can do to change our bodies in order to fit a socially constructed ideal, which is why this is so concerning. The only way we can address the damage this does is by teaching men to examine the issue critically and logically so that they may come to their own conclusion – it's not enough to just say 'the shape and size of your body doesn't matter', when virtually everywhere else they are being told the opposite. Men who feel emasculated by something entirely beyond their control are inclined to overcompensate elsewhere, and it's this that breeds unhealthy behaviour. Taking this anxiety over body image out of the equation might be the single most important step towards reducing toxic masculinity, but it's only achievable if all of us do our part.

How each of us can help

Ask yourself this: have you ever used someone's appearance to insult them? Of course you have, we all have and many continue to do so because it can be *so* easy and effective. If you haven't already, though, you must stop doing this immediately. It doesn't matter who the target is or how heinous an individual they may be: when you mock an unalterable aspect of their appearance, you're telling every innocent person who shares that characteristic that it's something to be embarrassed about. If you've followed news stories on Twitter about disgraced politicians such as Chris Christie or Rob Ford, you'll have seen endless jokes about their weight – for all their reprehensible behaviour and slimy personalities, people still choose to mock them for being fat, and believe that's okay because they're obviously bad men. By all means, criticise and insult them for the things that they've done – but don't bring their weight into this, it wasn't their bellies that did all those shitty things, because when you do you're mocking all overweight people and reinforcing the idea that their bodies are something to be embarrassed about.

I'm not saying you should avoid acknowledging beauty in conventionally attractive people for fear of reinforcing unrealistic ideas of body image, in fact, positive discussion of any physical attribute can be healthy in the right context. It's when you start talking about what's not attractive about a person that you need to consider stepping back; they may be wildly successful and probably won't even see your comments, let alone be fazed by them. But others might, and no matter how specific to your intended target they may be, the odds that no one else shares a similar feature are practically zero. Those who would never dream of making such comments to 'normal' men or women feel that insulting a celebrity's looks is justified, because these people tend to be constantly celebrated for their beauty by others, and one person's opinion to the contrary is insignificant as far as the target is concerned. This is probably true most of the time, but ignores the fact that it's still reinforcing to others the idea that certain physical qualities are objectively ugly or undesirable. You could take the most conventionally attractive person in the world, list every last thing that made them beautiful and it wouldn't make anyone else feel more ugly. You could take the very same person, find their flaws (because everyone has them), list them in the same way and probably leave someone feeling much more aware of their own imperfections. It doesn't matter who you're talking about, but *how* you're talking about them – as soon as things get negative, you risk doing damage.

The way in which women's bodies are portrayed in the media has been under scrutiny by campaigners – and the media itself – for some time now, and rightly so. More and more fashion shows have implemented bans on dangerously underweight models, mainstream retailers have started to accommodate women with fuller figures, and the Buzzfeeds of the world have covered the airbrushing of adverts and glamour shots from pretty much every imaginable angle. Obviously we've not come close to eliminating the practices that reinforce unrealistic expect-ations of body image, but on the whole we're definitely more aware of these issues than we were 20-odd years ago. One of the major driving forces behind this movement has been the mounting evidence that links such portrayals of beauty to psy-chological problems such as eating disorders in young women. It's not exactly a surprise that, in a world that tells girls they are defined by their looks while simultaneously showing them that beauty has a very narrow definition, women are growing up plagued by self-loathing and desperate to change anything they can to better fit society's idea of what's attractive. What makes disorders like anorexia so terrifying is that body dysmorphia – the inability to see how you truly look, even when looking in a mirror – prevents sufferers from ever being able to reach a point where they're satisfied with their weight, so once someone develops an eating disorder there's a very real chance they may never fully recover from it. Often, people who have ostensibly beaten eating disorders still have the same insecurities about their bodies years down the line, and though they are mentally strong enough to know they must continue overpowering such destructive impulses, the urges very much remain.

This is why it's so important that efforts are being made both medically and within our culture and media to tackle the onset of eating disorders; there is no sign of any real cure, and currently only prevention can reduce the number of sufferers. Historically, women have by far been the group most likely to develop some kind of eating disorder which is why they've been the major focus of recent campaigns. This is still the case today, but the rates in men are increasing sharply and it's possible that the media's focus on EDs as a female issue could be having unfortunate side effects for men. As we've already established, in general men are worse than women at talking about health issues: not only in terms of seeking help from their GP, but also their reluctance to open up to peers. (A friend recently pointed out that for women, intimate gynaecological exams are routine throughout their lives, so the whole experience is a lot more normal for them – men, on the other hand, don't tend to encounter doctors unless there's a serious problem, so are more embarrassed to do so.)

If men are unwilling to get help for ailments when there are no social connotations attached, then they're even more reluctant to do so when their illness is perceived as being feminine. The way eating disorders are framed as an overwhelmingly female problem is incredibly harmful to male sufferers, and those around them.

As far as Huw Oliver is concerned, the most important thing if we're to tackle these issues is better education about mental health more generally in Personal Social Health Education classes at school as well as in some form at universities. It should 'touch on all sorts of issues and include a diverse presentation of eating disorders as phenomena that can affect anyone, men included' in order to create a culture in which eating disorders can be discussed openly among peers and with sensitivity by staff. On top of that, more needs to be done to educated older generations, which Oliver would like to see happen via schools offering short mental health sessions with parents to explain the problems their children may face as they grow up. By not focusing on eating disorders in men, we risk sleepwalking into a situation in which it becomes as big and unpleasant a problem as it already is in women.

'As individuals, we just need to throw down all preconceptions we have of eating disorders and accept that men are equally susceptible to exactly the same set of mental health issues as women, including things like anorexia. And that means we need to be equally cognisant of their life-shattering potential in men and equally sympathetic towards sufferers of both sexes.'

For my money, we also need to look at why these insecurities exist in the first place and what makes them so powerful. When I asked Atkins, the personal trainer, what he thought motivated most men to go to gyms today, his answer was short but totally serious: 'To get laid.'

Man & Wife: Families, Personal Relationships and the Destructive Nature of Emotional Repression

> They fuck you up, your mum and dad.
>
> They may not mean to, but they do.
>
> They fill you with the faults they had
>
> And add some extra, just for you.

And so wrote Philip Larkin in the only Philip Larkin poem anyone actually knows. And he was right, you know.

Although none of this: these published words on paper, or screen, or in your ears if you chose the soothing Audiobook edition (which I can only hope you paid legitimate money for rather than torrenting or nicking from the book shop) would have happened were it not for a number of events in my personal life over the last decade and a bit, for your sake I've tried to keep the autobiographical stuff to a reasonable minimum up to this point. As much as I love the idea of taking tens of thousands of words to talk about myself, it seemed there were other, more pertinent avenues to explore around the subject of masculinity, and better individuals from which to draw than yours truly. That said, my ego can only give up so much attention, and since my family was such an important part in the creation of MAN UP, I figured it's only fair to devote a chapter to me and my kin – as well as looking at how families in general are affected by toxic masculinity today.

It wasn't until years after my dad died that any real discussion was had within my family about what turned out to be the most significant event in our lives. For my siblings and me, it was that most British of catalysts that ignited the conversation: alcohol. At a music festival aged 16, somewhere between dancing to A-Ha's 'Take On Me' (it was a Guilty Pleasures disco and I have no shame) and throwing up violently outside my tent, I first felt comfortable opening up to my older brother, Tom. We realised how closely each of our experiences mirrored the other's, right down to the bizarre dreams we occasionally had in which Dad appeared as if nothing had happened and gave some elaborate reason for his years-long absence. That night a bond we'd never previously had was built between us, something that continues to this day – and all it took was for me to be the most drunk I've ever been. With my sister, Sarah, the booze consumption was a little more staggered (to my liver's relief) but over a period of a few months her work brought her down to London on the odd weekend and we'd meet up, inevitably, in a pub. We laughed about how our mum had expressed concern to each of us about the other's drinking habits and realised that in our pessimism and low-level, self-destructive behaviour, we both take after our dad; I think we found it comforting to know we had this in common, and that it was perfectly okay not to be as relentlessly positive and well-meaning as our mother.

Around the ninth anniversary of Dad's death, Mum sent each of us a letter in which she shared her thoughts on how we dealt with the grief as a family. For the first time, she acknowledged that maybe we tried a little too hard to put on brave faces and go about our lives as if nothing had happened, but admitted it's easy to see such mistakes in retrospect and that at the time we did what we felt we had to. The one thing that really stuck with me was when she said that only the cats saw her break down crying at night, after we'd all gone to bed. I hadn't been so naïve as to think my mum wasn't in a great deal of pain, but it was a revelation to learn quite how intensely she'd struggled behind closed doors.

The format through which she broached the subject is of great significance: the written word gives you time to consider every thought and detail, and express these with a level of clarity rarely present in instant communication such as speech. When the subject matter is traumatic or upsetting, writing allows you to pause at any point and sort yourself out – at some point, we've all seen someone incapacitated by their emotions, trying and failing to speak through tears. You can say what you want to without any risk of interruption, and, above all, it provides enough detach-ment that you can discuss taboo issues which, frankly, it can feel too terrifying or humiliating to do in person. And letters – unlike emails or text messages – may take days to arrive, and recipients aren't bound by the same expectations to acknowledge or reply as they are with electronic communications. This is something I'll return to at the end of the book, but I imagine right now you're probably asking why I've gone off on this tangent and what it could possibly have to do with masculinity.

So yeah my dad died and it was a bit shit

As a quick recap for those who haven't been paying attention or for whatever reason decided to start halfway through, my dad died of a heart attack aged 51. The post-mortem revealed scar tissue from a previous attack, and it became apparent he had been suffering from pain when we found over-the-counter angina medication in his jacket pocket – something none of us knew about before. His refusal to show weakness in front of his family or to seek help from a doctor are classic characteristics of masculinity – and almost certainly a contributing factor in a death that could have been prevented. For whatever reason, he hid things from us. His intentions may have been noble – perhaps he didn't want to burden us with worry, for example – but the fact is, had he been more open, he might still be with us today.

It took my mother nine years before she was comfortable enough to admit to her children the true extent of her grief. The reason I went into such detail about the significance of letters is that I suspect even then she felt unable to speak about it directly, something I know well. The metaphor of 'opening up old wounds' really captures how reliving old trauma can be just as painful as it was at the time, particularly when done verbally. Personally, I have found it much easier to write about these issues as I am able to partially dissociate from them, while talking about them can sometimes be impossible. It took nine years before my pain was manageable enough to properly address. All that grief and sadness for something that didn't have to happen. My dad may have died from his masculinity, but it was his family who were the victims.

The impact an individual's behaviour can have on himself is one thing, but in reality it never stops just there. I've already explored the many ways in which toxic masculinity can damage a man, now we must look at its wider victims. Emotional repression, as we know, is a major factor contributing to poor mental health in men. It's not always a conscious decision, but when a man knowingly chooses not to confide in someone about an issue that's troubling him, he may try to rationalise this – believing it would be unfair to burden somebody else with his problems, for instance. This is something I have been guilty of in the past, even in situations where rationally I knew it would not be the case, I convinced myself otherwise. At its most extreme, this tendency to suffer in silence can lead to suicide, but even in low levels it can be damaging, particularly to romantic relationships. A man may think he's doing his partner a favour by not complaining, or believe he's reinforcing an attractive quality. 'Whining' is not a desirable or masculine trait, and many men understandably wish to avoid doing this, but unfortunately see their partaking in any kind of emotional discussion as falling under this umbrella definition. Whatever their reasons (if they have any) and no matter how small or insignificant an issue may be, over time this self-imposed silencing of troubling issues can leave their partner feeling shut out. Good relationships are built on trust and openness, and it doesn't matter how irrelevant a problem is to the partner – if you are unwilling to discuss it, it can breed emotional distance which, over time, can be irreparable. Again, this is something I have personal experience of.

Probably should have talked more

I suffered depression on and off, and in varying degrees of sever-ity, from roughly around the time adolescence began to set in. For the last couple of years my mental health has been, largely, in good shape, but I don't want to hedge my bets and put an end date on my illness when I know that there's every chance it could resurface again at any point in the future. If you look closely at the top of my left arm, near the shoulder, you can still see the scars from where I went through a period of cutting myself in my early teens. That's a fact about myself few of my immedi-ate family or friends will have known up to this point and may continue to be oblivious to, on account of the fact that they'll probably have given up on this book several chapters ago after being bored nearly to death. The positioning of these scars is more significant than perhaps you'd imagine. Like many people who self-harm, I did it for the cathartic release it provides. I was also worried that if anyone found out, they'd think I was just attention-seeking, so ensured I cut only areas that could easily be hidden by short sleeved shirts.

My depression was at its worst in my early twenties and coincided with my first proper, long-term relationship. I knew that the way I had dealt (or failed to deal) with my mental health issues was certainly a catalyst in the eventual collapse of the relationship, but curious to find out how exactly, I gave my ex, Megan, free reign to talk about my flaws. Honestly, I was kind of disappointed by how kind her response was, though it did reveal some important stuff about myself.

For the first portion of our relationship, one of the major hurdles we faced was my complete inability to open up. If there was ever any tension between us over something Megan had said or done to inadvertently piss me off, I struggled to articulate it or just shrugged it off, meaning I stayed angry and she was unable to understand what, in terms of habits or behaviours, I found annoying because I simply didn't tell her what bothered me. I certainly didn't open up about emotional issues for a very long time, so even though I was clearly dealing with a lot of anguish, I would avoid discussing it, and my girlfriend would be forced to tiptoe around me and tolerate my foul moods because I wasn't comfortable speaking about what I was experiencing. As time went on, she encouraged me to come out of my shell a bit, and I got better at sharing the deeper details of my life with her, but there was a catch: only with her. This meant that every problem I had, every grievance, the only person who'd hear it would be Megan. She became a metaphorical punching bag, single-handedly having to deal with my shit because I felt unable to talk to anyone else. I don't think she ever resented me for this – though she'd have probably been justified if she had – but it put an enormous strain on our relationship and sucked out an awful lot of joy.

Like the notorious woman abuser* John Lennon once said, all you need is love

When you start preaching the importance of love, you end up sounding like a bit of a dickhead. 'Hey man, it's the 60s, let's

* He didn't shy away from it either, as he told *Playboy* in 1980: 'I used to be cruel to my woman, and physically - any woman. I was a hitter. I couldn't express myself and I hit. I fought men and I hit women.'

all be really chill and cool and not hate, only love' – oh fuck off, why don't you? It also tends to come across as a bit of an empty gesture: like yeah, we know love is great, but it's not going to solve all the world's problems is it? But if you can get past the hippies and those annoying pricks who stand in town centres holding signs that read 'free hugs', you can start to see that love is so crucial in all of our lives.

My dad was not a bad person by any means. He supported and cared for his family, he was around way more than other people's dads, he was funny and kind and wildly intelligent. He wasn't, however, very good at showing his love – at least not in an open, vocal way. It wasn't his fault he was like this, he had grown up with a father whose war-trauma and subsequent drinking problem left him unable to express any real emotions, so my dad learned that this was the way men should act.

I know that I, of all people, should not be surprised at how pervasive toxic masculinity can be, but I am still shocked by certain things I witness or read. In the past year I've encountered (online) multiple men who are uncomfortable with the idea of kissing or hugging their sons for fear of encouraging homosexual thoughts in them. These aren't isolated incidents: there is a genuine belief amongst some people that fathers shouldn't physically express love for their male children. The internet is awash with comments such as this: 'Fathers, stop kissing your sons on the mouth! You're subconsciously blurring gender lines.'[30] Stop and think about that for a moment. There are men who would rather their sons grow up unable to show love and affection than grow up gay.

This kind of thinking hurts so many people. It hurts the

sons, who feel unloved by the people who should love them the most. It hurts gay people by breeding homophobia and stigmatising any kind of positive same sex interactions. It hurts anyone whose lives ever intersect with the lives of these boys: their male friends, who feel unable to reach out emotionally in times of need; their partners, who may not be shown the regular affection they want and need; their own children, who will follow in their father's footsteps.

Years after Dad died, I learned that towards the end of his life, his marriage to my mum wasn't as happy as it had always been. It's hardly surprising: you're going to have problems when you spend several decades with any person, but it certainly wasn't beyond repair (until he went and died, that is – way to blow it, Dad). I found this out around the time Megan and I broke up, my mum revealed it to me in a letter prompted by the sort of concerns mothers have about their children when they're going through a rough patch. Mum told me that the hardest thing about being married to my dad was that he was so poor at showing his love – for both her and us kids – and while she never doubted that he loved her dearly, he so rarely expressed this. Reading that letter, I suddenly saw so much of myself in my father, and some of the parallels between their marriage and my relationship with Megan were eerily similar. One of the other complaints Megan had about our time together was that she found me unable to express affection in a sincere manner: I would always hide it behind jokes or quips. It makes sense that I behaved this way, having grown up with a father who never really felt comfortable displaying affection to either his wife or children.

Sons become their fathers become their sons

The bond between fathers and sons is uniquely powerful. I don't mean to say the bond is necessarily good or healthy: the relationship can have an intense effect on boys regardless of this. Despite what a boy is capable of learning from his mother, he will look to his father to see how to act and follow his lead quite possibly by instinct. How often do we hear that boys, particularly those raised by single mothers, need strong male role models if they're to grow up to be decent people? It's true that men take after men in a unique way – they're more willing to learn from other men or trust other men or consume art made by other men – so a lot of the time, the way a man behaves is probably guided by the way his father behaved. And this is worrying.

When my paternal grandfather returned to England after fighting in the second world war, he was barely a functioning human. Like so many, he'd been forced to witness horrific, disturbing things repeatedly, humanity at its most depraved. He was utterly traumatised and began drinking heavily, presumably as a means of escape, suppressing his own memories. The term 'Post-Traumatic Stress Disorder' had not yet been coined, and our understanding of mental health was comparatively primitive, with soldiers encouraged to adopt a stiff upper lip – something we now know is unhealthy. For those like my grandfather, dealing with PTSD, their only treatment option was to self-medicate and to try to avoid talking or thinking about the experience. It's a story familiar to many people whose loved ones served: 'He never spoke of the war.'

To some extent, my dad was lucky in his upbringing. His father's PTSD and alcoholism manifested itself passively for the most part; others in similar situations faced physical violence and suffered quite painful childhoods. Domestic abuse and masculinity have a complicated but inescapable relationship. Of course anyone can be an abuser, not just men, and there are innumerable factors behind the presence of abusive behaviour. Toxic masculinity is just one, but I would argue it's an important one to look at.

Power, dominance, control and violence are all traits we would associate with masculinity. Depending on the context in which they're present, they can also all be traits of abusive behaviour. By this point, you should be familiar with the basic definition of toxic masculinity: exaggerated behaviour intended to make oneself appear more masculine, usually prompted by insecurities, usually detached from the positive, genuine expression of masculinity it's trying to mimic. When men feel emasculated, they respond by attempting to claw back a sense of masculinity any way they can. Unfortunately, this can have dire consequences for others around them.

At times of economic hardship, domestic violence soars – something that is usually attributed to a general rise in stress. Although I have no reason to doubt this explanation, I do think these spikes in domestic violence warrant a closer, more focused look at causes beyond stress alone. I previously wrote about how globalisation and capitalism in the 20th century commodified masculinity and forged a link between a man's wealth and his manhood, as well as the hopelessness and emasculation of long-term unemployment, both of which I feel are relevant here. In a society that ascribes masculinity to money or employment, men who suddenly find themselves without one or both can easily feel their manliness is under threat. And we know where this can lead.

Abusers come in all shapes and sizes, and are not limited to any gender or social group. So does abuse itself: physical abuse is just one variety, but other abuse might be perpetrated on an entirely emotional level, or verbally. Verbal and emotional abuse are harder to identify or prove, than physical abuse, which can be more evident and also more immediately terrifying to the victim, which probably explains why it is the physical kind that tends to be reported to police far more frequently. Emotional abuse may be drawn out over a long period, and while the same is also true of physical abuse, the latter may flare up in a more clear, defined way – an attack may be triggered when the perpetrator loses their temper, for instance. Men are significantly more likely to be physically violent than women – a quick glance at the gender breakdown of violent crime stats is more than enough to back this up – which means that any time we see a spike in domestic violence we can safely assume most of the perpetrators are male.

Because abuse by its very nature is senseless and inexcusable, I'm not comfortable with the idea of saying anything causes it per se – particularly not the actions of victims – and the blame must lie solely with the abuser. There are certain triggers we can look at, however, which reveal the extent of the link between abuse and toxic masculinity. There tends to be an emotional reason for most violent outbursts: abusers generally don't lash out if they're in a good mood. At its most primal, violence is an expression of a negative emotional state – anger, sadness, frustration – feelings everyone is familiar with. Several chapters back, I brought up the idea of two kinds of toxic masculinity: active and passive. Healthy men talk about their emotions openly. Some men bottle everything up, express nothing – a passive form of toxic masculinity. Violence is an active form of toxic masculinity, a harmful way of channelling emotional issues in a manner that's perceived as masculine.

Jealousy is a common trait in abusive relationships, and a cheating spouse is regularly used as an excuse in assault or murder trials, colloquially referred to as the 'cuckold's defence' – it was only a few years ago that Britain stopped allowing this as a valid defence in court. An overwhelming amount of the time, such murders are committed by men with female victims. What does this tell us about abuse and masculinity? Well, for one, that society still views women as belonging to men, as our property – and the reason the cuckold's defence has been permitted historically is because men are forgiven their 'crime of passion' if it's in retaliation to the ultimate pain: emasculation. Indeed, 'cuckold' by its very definition refers to the husband of an adulteress, never the wife of an adulterer, in case you weren't already clear on the one-sidedness of this. Just as the economy can affect domestic violence rates by encouraging feelings of (emasculated) hopelessness, jealousy is another example of how destructive and evil men can be when they perceive their masculinity as being under threat.

The unintentional consequences of toxic masculinity

The effects of toxic masculinity on a man's family don't end with his direct actions or teachings. Had my dad been more willing to ask for help, more comfortable telling my mum about his health problems, I strongly believe he may not have died when he did. Quite literally, he put the 'toxic' in 'toxic masculinity'.

About three weeks before my 10th birthday, as the chicken roasted for our Sunday dinner, my dad collapsed in the down-stairs bathroom of our family home. I waited outside the house to flag down the first paramedics, and we were ushered off to the neighbour's house. Eventually Mum came back and told us he hadn't made it, and we returned to the kitchen where he'd been laid on the floor. One thing that really stuck with me was the way his eyes were half open, not closed like in films, staring blankly out as we kneeled over him. The older I get, the less I remember from my childhood, but the sight of my father's body is as clear today as it ever was. I still get dreams, less frequently than I used to, where he's somehow alive – and it still hurts when I wake up and lose him all over again.

Seeing a loved one die as a child, it turns out, can mess you up a bit. I may sound like a broken record bringing suicide up again, but as I already established it's probably the biggest issue facing men today. I'm always a little reluctant to say we should prioritise a reduction in the male suicide rate above all other aspects of toxic masculinity, because it runs the risk of putting men's lives before everyone else's. Why not first tackle deadly male violence against women? After all, suicide is just what men are doing to themselves, right?

When someone dies, they are generally the person who is least affected by their death, on account of the fact that they're dead and no longer have to think about anything much at all. When toxic masculinity factors into a man taking his own life, he is a victim of his toxic masculinity. But he is only *a* victim of his toxic masculinity, and not *the* victim. The toxic masculinity doesn't die with him, it moves on to his friends and family and anyone who ever cared about him. Often, the hardest hit by male suicide are women and children. Bereavement of any kind can be traumatic for the deceased's loved ones, suicide even more so. Families are forced to question if there was anything they could have done, burdened with guilt and, above all, faced with the knowledge that this death – unlike the deaths of those who succumb to natural causes – was preventable.

How can we fix this?

The Men's Rights movement is, as far as I'm concerned, deplorable: hijacking important issues for a largely misogynistic agenda of its own. That said, some of the causes it claims to stand for are not entirely without merit. One such example is the lack of support available for male victims of domestic violence, who are indeed underrepresented and often ignored. I would love to see action on this front, but the cold hard reality is that resources are limited and women are still much more likely to be victims than men. Throughout the book, I have returned to the idea that many problems facing men today could be addressed through the very fight for equality in which feminists are currently engaged, and this is the case here. It's not enough to provide the victims of domestic violence with shelter and protection if we are not going to tackle the roots of this violence on a social and cultural level. It is *always* better to prevent the disease than to treat it. Why are men so quick to resort to violence? What are the psychological reasons for this? What are the risk factors? How can we better rehabilitate men convicted of domestic violence?

I refuse to believe that we, as a society, are unable to reduce male-perpetrated domestic violence by working together and moulding healthier behaviour across all facets of masculinity. Yes, in the short term we need more resources for victims of any gender, but if we play the long game we might actually be able to make progress. If Men's Rights Activists focused all their energy on changing the attitudes that make domestic violence so prevalent, a drop in the overall rate of these incidents would mean more time and money could be devoted to the male victims they claim to care about. But that's not what MRAs are about. They seek to divide us by gender, to perpetuate inequality, and to attack women. Men's Rights is a misnomer, for these people are less concerned with helping men than hurting women. In common with the stated cause of the MRAs, I believe that men are victims of gender inequality. Unlike the MRAs, I find the notion that inequality can be resolved by further inequality absurd.

The harm wrought by an expression of toxic masculinity is never confined to the man in which it's present. Humans are highly social creatures; any behaviour we exhibit inevitably touches the lives of others, for better or worse. Naturally, it's those closest to us who have to shoulder the majority of this – our families, in most cases. Toxic masculinity prevents us from doing some of the most primal human things. It stops us showing our loved ones love. It leaves our partners feeling unappreciated and worthless, and teaches our sons to follow our lead. It builds barriers to communication – the single most important thing for a good relationship – shuts out from our lives the only people who truly care, destabilises, weakens bonds, brings dissatisfaction and unhappiness to both sides. It destroys logical thought, creates a mindset that prioritises pride, dignity and stoicism over such basic needs as our health (it killed my father this way, fucking me up for several years). It prevents us from expressing emotions in a healthy, vocal manner, which can result in one of two outcomes: we either bottle up all our problems and let them slowly wreck us from the inside, becoming hopeless and, in extreme cases, suicidal; or we resort to violence, taking out our anger and frustration on our innocent families.

You may remember from a few chapters back the story Jonny Sharples told about his brother Simon's suicide. This is how it affected his family:

'Simon's death had a huge impact on our family; our immediate family had five huge personalities in it for twenty-eight years but for the past twelve months it's only had four – when we get together then there is always the air that somebody is missing, there's one less smile in our photographs and one less laugh around the dinner table. I think perhaps sometimes you take your family for granted, as much as you wish you didn't, but they're the people that you saw every day of your life for eighteen years or so – you really feel it when one of them disappears. I think of Simon every day; I wish he was around to see my nephew's first day at school, I wish he could have gone to Wembley to watch Preston North End win, I wish he was around to meet my girlfriend. There's so many things that cross my mind about how things would be different now if he was still here, and I'm sure my family would all say the same thing and have their own personal wishes about what Simon could have witnessed, but I know we all treasure the photographs we have of Simon and more importantly I know we all cherish the memories we have of him – thankfully not even his passing can take those away from us.'

Toxic masculinity kills, whether it be through suicide, as in the case of Simon Sharples or pride and fear, as with my dad – and not just ourselves, either. And for what? This is the most difficult thing to comprehend. It might also be the biggest reason for a lot of people to start giving a shit about toxic masculinity. I lost my father when I was nine years old. I was there in the house when he died, I stood outside to flag down the paramedics, I sat in silence with my siblings at a neighbour's house more scared than I'd ever been and felt my world turn upside down when our mum arrived and broke the news. I saw his body laid out on the kitchen floor, stared into his half-closed eyes, stroked our family cat as she sat whimpering on his chest, and watched as the paramedics hauled him into a black bag and wheeled him away from his home for the last time. I dreamt about him regularly for years, and on occasion still do. Years later, those dreams are no less painful to wake up from.

I had a good childhood after he died, my mum made sure of that. Sometimes, though, I struggled. I occasionally went to the football with two or three mates and their dads, and slightly resented what they had and took for granted. One of the few memories I have of me and Dad alone together was an evening match at Filbert Street, Leicester City's old ground. He bought us each one of those awful sport-stadium hotdogs, which I wolfed down with a thrill after he made me promise not to tell

Mum we'd eaten them. Every now and again I just wanted him back for a couple of hours so we could do something mundane, like all the other kids did with their dads.

As a family we didn't deal with the grief in a particularly healthy way, we just sort of got on with our lives and avoided the subject as best we could. It's easy to look back on it though, and at the time we did what felt right to us, and I don't blame or resent anyone for how we went about it. I have no doubt this played a big role in how I dealt with emotional issues as I grew older though, and the periods of depression I went through in my teens and early twenties were almost certainly exacerbated by my inability to open up. I've lived a comfortable, relatively happy life and don't want this to come off as a sob story, but the truth is my dad's death did a lot of damage to me and my family. I'm not angry at him or blaming him – that said, every now and again I do wonder *what if things had been different?* and more so than that, simply *why?* We live in a world where men are somehow convinced that being perceived as masculine is more important than literally anything, including their lives. Worse yet, our definitions of masculinity have become so warped and removed from any positive purpose, that in our attempts to attain it, widespread destructive behaviour in males is now inevitable.

I started writing about masculinity in the vain hope someone could be spared what I went through. My dad's death fucked me up. I can barely begin to fathom how painful it must be to lose someone to suicide, or to be the victim of domestic violence. Toxic masculinity is *incomprehensibly* damaging to families. Did my dad die for his sense of manhood? Yes, I believe so. Do other men bring trauma to loved ones for theirs? Definitely. And for what? My dad had maybe a few months of embarrassment-free living, and upheld his pride through not complaining about his chest pains or, god forbid, relinquishing his independence by seeing a doctor. He got to feel like more of a man for a short while, and in return I got to grow up without my dad. It might sound like I'm blaming him or calling him selfish, but I'm not. Selfish is a word that's also used often by misinformed people to describe the act of suicide, but again this is wrong. And while there is no defending the perpetrators of domestic violence or their heinous actions, the prevalence of these crimes, their common traits and associated trends does suggest the presence of outside influences.

My dad was a smart man. He worked as a chemist for a fairly big pharmaceuticals company, before becoming a sales rep – he knew his shit when it came to health care, it was literally his job to talk about it. He was a member of Mensa, briefly, and a talented artist – many of his paintings still hang on the walls at home. He was by no means a conformist – as his fashion sense would demonstrate – and was capable of making his own decisions for the most part. So how did this man end up dying of something he knew was a problem and could be prevented?

Well, sometimes society is just too damn strong.

All of us humans are influenced to a degree by our environment, some more so than others. Fashion, culture, food, politics – we all look to others for guidance. Conforming to societal norms is what keeps us from anarchy, the existence of civilised society and general politeness is proof enough that most of us are sheep. We want to fit in and be liked and respected, it provides us with a sense of security, and might be our strongest remaining link to our early tribal ancestors. As men, we're taught from birth that the most important thing in our lives is our masculinity.

Everyone is guilty of perpetuating this. Even feminists who I would expect to know better will reply to abuse from trolls by calling them virgins or suggesting they have small dicks, both of which are so closely associated with masculinity (or lack thereof) that the intention is to shame them for not being man enough. It's tempting to react this way, because it obviously hits men hard, but I still think it would be healthier for people to stop doing this. As long as society tells men so ubiquitously that the most important thing they have to strive for is masculinity, men like my dad will continue to respond to their insecurities in needlessly damaging ways. The biggest victims of toxic masculinity are not men, but their families. Time and time again, women and children are left to pick up the pieces and deal with immense trauma because society told a loved one to put his masculinity first.

To any men reading this, I urge you to question your priorities, and hope you realise how senseless it is to risk anything in order to feel like more of a man – if not for your own sake, then for the sake of your partners, families, friends. Masculinity isn't a constant: it can fluctuate, you can't lose it irredeemably. You're allowed moments of what our culture might consider 'weakness' – in fact, you should embrace them, because often they'll give you the power to bounce back stronger than ever. Masculinity isn't a finite thing – but a human life is.

And to anyone, regardless of gender, who wants to reduce the harm wrought by toxic masculinity, I ask that you lead by example and question your words and actions. It may seem insignificant to counter trolls with insults intended to hit their sense of masculinity, but every time anyone does this, it sends the message that masculinity is the most important thing a man should strive for. If a few less people did that on a regular basis, then maybe men could start to think more objectively and not take deadly risks while blinded by our society's false standards.

Masculinity Beyond (Straight) Men: The Impact on Women's Rights and the LGBT Movement

Unless my writing has been entirely unclear up to this point – and to be fair, there's every chance of this being the case – you should now be reasonably familiar with the notion that masculinity is a potent ideal towards which men (and even, to an extent, women and others) are encouraged to aspire. And while definitions of masculinity do differ from person to person, culture to culture and time to time, one of the qualities often most strongly associated with manliness relates to sexuality – specifically, being straight.

Sexuality is a weird facet of masculinity and does a decent job of highlighting the arbitrary way we tend to assign these qualities. After all, there's no ostensible reasons why 'straight' should equal 'masculine', and in 2016 the idea that gay men are incapable of being incredibly manly has gone the way of the malicious rumour that my 13-year-old self was responsible for creating the email address jack_urwin_iz_fit@hotmail.com: that is to say, I am sure some people still believe this is the case, but they are objectively wrong. So why, in a great deal of readings of gender, does heterosexuality still factor into masculinity?

Because it's the default. Straight is the default for everyone – gay women 'come out' just as gay men do – but it hits men harder because masculinity is so highly prized. Thanks to feminism and the general progress women's rights have seen, girls are being encouraged to pursue careers in more traditionally masculine (or at least male dominated) fields – if not by their friends and family just yet, then by big names in media. By contrast, boys aren't pushed nearly as much to go into female-dominated areas. Although I understand the necessity to reach out to girls like this, especially because those male-dominated jobs are likely to pay better, it does seem to suggest that masculinity confers far more advantages. Straight may be the default for everyone, but it carries a lot more weight for males.

Anyone who doesn't conform to the heterosexual ideal of masculinity with which our society is most familiar is hurt. So who are the non-conformists? To start with, gay people. Traditional gender roles are based around family, and by exten- sion, procreation – anyone who deviates from heterosexual relationships does not conform to these ideals. Transgender or non-binary people, because their gender identity does not match their biological sex, and again, they don't conform to gender roles. Feminists, or, in fact, any woman who wants financial independence. They're seen as having betrayed their roles, and also as being threats to men for doing all the things we used to do alone. In short: anyone who doesn't tick all the stereo- typical boxes with which their gender is associated: plenty of straight men, for example, face ridicule from their own kind for having unusual hobbies or interests. But those most affected are women and LGBT people.

In the last couple of years, one of the most frequently recurring memes I've seen do the rounds on Facebook and Twitter is a quote about homophobia – sometimes falsely attributed to Morgan Freeman, probably because everything sounds more insightful when you imagine it spoken by that soothing baritone: 'I hate the word homophobia. It's not a phobia. You are not scared. You are an asshole.'

This crops up in some form every few weeks in the seemingly universal context of support for gay rights, although I'm sure there are some dark corners of the internet where it's somehow been hijacked by homophobes (it's the fucking internet after all). It's not exactly difficult to understand why it's so popular: as society's acceptance of homosexuality continues to grow and supporters become ever more vocal, much of the fight against homophobia centres on pointing out the absurd, arbitrary reasons for disliking gay people and ridiculing such opinions. Plenty of the opposition to LGBT people does indeed stem from individuals simply being dicks, and perhaps there should be a specific term for this to reflect the fact, but homophobia (in its most literal definition as an irrational fear or hatred of homosexuals or homosexuality) *does* exist, and in a much bigger way than the popularity of this meme would suggest many people realise.

The defining issue of the gay rights movement in the west this millennium – or, at least, the one that's received most coverage – has been same-sex marriage. In several countries, the UK included, the battle has already been won and people are free to marry whomever they please regardless of gender. However, this hasn't happened without a great deal of resistance from politicians and the public alike, many of whom – while maintaining they were in no way homophobic – argued that it went against (largely religious) definitions of traditional marriage. In an attempt to persuade politicians to vote in favour, many supporters of equal marriage asked them to consider how their decision will appear to future generations, suggesting a vote against would place them, shamefully, on 'the wrong side of history'. In the US this has carried a particular weight because it is so reminiscent of the ban on interracial marriage that was struck down in 1967. Now, half a century later, those who voted in favour of keeping the ban are viewed as the misguided fools (if not all-out hateful bigots) that they were. Even the most hard-right, evangelical, gay-hating politicians in the US would not publicly hold such an opinion today.

The parallels drawn between the two movements are helpful for studying current shifts in opinion and providing context for the present; widespread support for gay rights didn't come about until relatively recently, but civil rights regarding race have a much longer history and so can teach us a lot about opinions on LGBT issues today.

Returning for a second to that quote about homophobia that Morgan Freeman didn't say: consider it reworked into the context of race. Obviously, you can't simply replace 'homophobia' with 'racism' because racism doesn't mean a fear of other races, but the point would still stand that racists are not afraid, they're assholes. When we think of racism at its most extreme, we tend to think of groups like the Ku Klux Klan, responsible for countless brutal murders of people on the basis of skin colour. Black people have been terrorised in America from the time they first arrived as slaves, right up to the present day. Racially motivated killings of black people outnumber racially motivated killings of white people by other races on an extraordinary scale. It's well documented that the judicial system in America is racist, with African Americans locked up many times more than white Americans for the same crimes; the Black Lives Matter movement that began after Michael Brown's death in Ferguson in August 2014 was set up to protest the shockingly frequent killings of unarmed black men by police and the attendant lack of consequences, with cops rarely facing trial even when there's significant evidence against them. Historically, fear has bred racism. Many white people viewed blacks as savages: they were perceived as being naturally predisposed towards criminal behaviour and treated as a non-human species. Today, yes, most racists are assholes, but this widespread fear persists – I've read and been told of many instances in which black men, walking down the street, have witnessed a white person coming towards them cross the road and then return to the other side shortly after, for no discernible reason, but the men know why: people are afraid of black men.

Now, what's this got to do with homophobia? After all, it's not as if gay people have been stereotyped as violent criminals. Homophobes aren't afraid, they're just assholes right? Wrong. Homophobia is real, and what's more, even the most vocal supporters of gay rights can be guilty of this. It's real, it's common, and it's mostly a problem perpetuated by straight men and their ideas of masculinity.

Back in school, 'gay' was a word that carried enormous connotations even before we really understood the concept of sexuality. It was thrown around constantly as an all-purpose insult between boys without any real sense of the damage this could do; as a result, I think most men have at some point in their lives found themselves acting in a particular way for fear of being branded as such. As I touched upon in chapter 4, there are few things more important in our formative years than popularity – specifically, fitting in – and on some level this breeds a sort of self-preservationist behaviour. We may well be aware that sucking up to the cool kids and pretending that we're something we're not isn't exactly healthy, but the desire not to be at the bottom of the social pile or singled out as a target for both emotional and physical abuse is a powerful motivator. Bullying can have such a profound effect on a person's life, and the reasons for this are much broader than the obvious, direct trauma: victims frequently become isolated and lose friends they once had, because of the threat of facing the same attacks as a result of simply being associated with the victim. When 'acting gay' is one of the things most likely to get you taunted or beaten up, it's hardly surprising that most boys will do whatever they can to appear straight.

This raises one of the most crucial questions about masculinity, itself a major part of answering the very question we set out to achieve in the beginning of MAN UP: what does 'straight' look like? For young boys (and indeed plenty of grown men), the answer is 'the opposite of gay'. In this day and age, it's abundantly clear (I hope) to any adult with half a brain that the one definition of a gay man is an attraction to other men.

However, for kids, the homophobic bullying starts long before any sexual awakening, and it's not at all uncommon for school age children to be bullied as 'gay' without having ever expressed any attraction to the same sex (for boys who are certain of, or questioning their attraction to men, it's rarely something they share for fear of the consequences). The fact is, at this stage 'acting gay' is synonymous with looking or behaving effeminate, or sometimes simply for deviating from societal norms of masculinity in any way. It might be the way you dress, your haircut, your voice, your hobbies, your emotional availability, even the way you walk – pretty much every aspect of your body and mind can be interpreted as proof of your sexuality, however absurd it may be. And that's if there is even 'a reason' – much of the power established at this age comes from ostracisation and 'othering', and sexuality can be merely a handy tool by which this is enforced. Regardless, you're risking a miserable few years if you don't adapt to fit the picture of what a straight man should be, so that is what most boys do. This isn't necessarily something we do out of malice or ill-feelings towards gay people, and it in no way prevents us from growing up as accepting individuals, it is merely something we do as a survival mechanism. The behaviour does tend to become second nature though, and regardless of what we may believe in later life, the habits drilled into us at such a young age can be difficult to shake.

Homophobic behaviour in a person often begins not as a hatred of gay people, but as a punishment for deviating from our societal perception of masculinity. You don't need to be gay to be the victim of homophobic bullying (but it probably helps). Heterosexual men can feel the need to state their sexuality, sometimes, rather ironically, at the same time as discussing how cool they are with the concept of LGBT people. There are a variety of reasons for this – for instance, they might worry a woman they're hoping to impress will assume their openness about gay people is because they themselves are gay, and unless they clarify to the contrary, they've cockblocked themselves. Often it's something you see when they're actually in the company of gay people, believing themselves to be irresistible and fearing endless unwanted advances, perhaps even paranoid that after a few drinks they'll be taken advantage of. In their minds, the fact they are socialising with gay men is proof that they're totally cool about LGBT issues – but if they also feel the need to carry themselves differently to how they would if surrounded by straight people, they are in the very literal sense of the word, homophobic. (It's more than possible that this fear stems from the way straight men treat women and how they react when they find themselves occupying the positions in which they've placed women in the past.) Even when men aren't vocally expressing their heterosexuality, so much of the way we behave can be linked to this same need to appear unambiguously straight: think about how many men you personally know who don't own a single item of pink clothing, and how many times you've heard a man in your life say he doesn't like the colour of a shirt because it's an effeminate colour and makes him look gay. 'Not that there's anything wrong with that!' they say, 'I just don't personally want people to think I'm that way!'

This can all seem insignificant and harmless in the general scheme of things, but every little thought like this contributes over time to a stereotype that's totally false, and reinforces that idea of what homosexuality looks like to the next generation of school bullies – and that's something much bigger than the colour of a man's shirt. Sure, no one gets directly hurt when we joke that an item of clothing makes a man 'look gay', but the message it sends is that gay men really can be defined by something other than their sexuality. To an impressionable mind, if a shirt can be gay, then so can just about anything. The way in which gay men are stereotyped as having feminine characteristics, means they can face similar discrimination in certain areas of life. Take careers for example: gay men, like women, are often seen as being overly emotional, something that's perceived as a weakness in high-stress (and often manual) jobs, so can lose out on roles because of their sexuality.

In the gay community, there are a few words – embraced by some, hated by others for the binary notions they impose – used as labels to refer to men who are either traditionally masculine, or more effeminate in the way they present themselves. 'Femmes' or 'twinks' in many ways reflect historical stereotypes of gay men as less masculine – for some men, this is a way of directly pushing back against the hypermasculine behaviour they felt forced to display before they came out; or the words might simply be a true representation of their personalities (in which, unlike straight men, they can be comfortable). 'Masc' gay guys or 'bears' are personalities that conform more with what our traditional idea of masculinity looks like. But like gender itself, these terms are extreme examples. See, it turns out that gay men are no different, in all but one way, to straight men – but many people refuse to believe that our sexuality doesn't define us. Attitudes are improving and anti-discrimination laws in many western countries aim to prevent people being treated differently because of false perceptions about who or what they might be, but our inherent homophobia continues to be a big problem.

When a friend came out to me in our teens, after several pitchers of beer, he told me: 'Don't worry, I don't fancy you or anything.' It's something that's stayed with me for a long time, that even though he knew he could trust me and that I wouldn't think differently of him in any way, he felt he had to qualify it with a reassurance he didn't find me attractive. This wasn't something I had remotely considered and I told him, only half-jokingly, that I was offended to hear I don't have universal sex appeal, but it was clearly something he had felt was necessary to clarify. I have come to realise since then that his need to tell me this had a totally reasonable foundation: we, as a society, often perceive gay men as being sex-obsessed with no self control and few morals, and a decent number of straight men – having extraordinarily inflated egos – struggle to believe that gay men are not attracted to them. Again, there is a very real possibility that they are basing these prejudices on their own behaviour: most lesbians have at some point faced harassment by men who claim they can 'turn' them, trying to convince the women in question that they just 'haven't been with the right man'. In the eyes of these straight guys, gay men are attracted to *all* men and unless they make it clear how completely heterosexual they are, the attention from gays will be relentless. It's easy to laugh at such baseless insecurities, until you realise the consequences they can have, including, in some parts of the world, legal justification for murder.

'Gay panic defence' can be used by defendants in assault or murder cases who have been the object of homosexual romantic or sexual advances so frightening to them that it brought on a psychotic state characterised by unusual violence. There is absolutely no scientific evidence to support the existence of this supposed psychiatric condition, and as a result it's been ruled inadmissible in many jurisdictions, but is still legal in parts of Australia and the United States. It was only in September 2014 that California became the first state to ban the defence. In November 2009, the New Zealand parliament removed the provocation defence from New Zealand Law (abolishing it from the country's Crimes Act of 1961), but a mere four months earlier the gay panic defence had been used successfully to downgrade a murder charge to manslaughter. Such a defence would seem utterly backwards even a century ago; the fact it's still being used today is stunning, but it shows us quite how deep-rooted our homophobia is. There is no equivalent law in place regarding heterosexual advances, which would serve largely as a defence for women, considering how the vast majority of unwanted sexual advances that leave the target intimidated or scared are made towards women, by men. By contrast, every single use of the gay panic defence has been by a male defendant. When they feel their very masculinity is being threatened, straight men can be capable of horrific actions. The way we are forced from such an early age to adhere to a strict gender binary – if you're assigned male at birth, you're a boy, no questions – and the emphasis on masculinity in particular, shapes everyone's life. But perhaps no group suffers as harshly from this as transgender people. I've spent much of this book exploring how hypermasculinity harms cis men by pushing them to unhealthy and, usually, arbitrary extremes of behaviour and attitude; but consider what that hypermasculinity can do to young trans women who have yet to come out publicly or even to themselves.

Homophobia ruins the lives of gay people. It's often deadly, in fact, motivating both murder and suicide. I'm making a note of this now in the hope that what I say next doesn't come off as trivialising the LGBT victims of homophobia or suggesting we should make this issue all about straight people. But homophobia is one of the earliest forces that conditions, and very often damages straight people too, particularly males. Boys, especially when they're in peer-driven environments like schools, fear others will think they're gay. They're taught to push out any remotely 'effeminate' mannerisms or activities, to conceal their emotions, and ditch anything, or anyone, that might raise questions about their sexuality. They learn to treat women as mere objects that exist for their own pleasure, and are discouraged from forming platonic bonds with them (after all, the boy whose friends are predominantly girls *cannot* be straight), and by doing so at such a crucial age, they fail to grasp the appropriate way to treat women and shut themselves off from the only people left in this environment who are likely to give a damn about their emotional problems and help them talk things through. They're forced to sacrifice hobbies they're genuinely interested in, choose subjects at school that aren't seen as girly – hell, pursue careers they don't really like because of a system that makes us decide the path our futures take before we're even old enough to drink. All to not look gay.

Séan Faye is a non-binary transgender person, assigned

male at birth and raised as a boy. 'I don't identify with either the category "man" or "woman" fully. If you were to put me on a scale between the two I'm closer to femininity and woman-hood in my mode of dress and my identity. I ask people to use the gender-neutral pronouns "they/them" as a preference, but will settle for "she" as a rule.' Faye has experienced first-hand the way toxic masculinity hurts LGBT people, having spent their formative years in all-boys school.

'It was a macho culture – albeit a very middle class, public-schooly type of macho. A lot of male posturing, defi-nitely, but everyone was a middle class boy who wanted to do well academically and came from money (except those of us on scholarships). It's very odd because I *picked* an all-male school at 10 but had no conception of what that meant until I got there. I didn't hate my time at school, but it was truly a schooling in how different I was to the vast majority of my peers. I took the changes of puberty very hard, and it was harder still being around other male teens who seemed to perform their puberty in similar ways – rowdiness, preoccupation with sex and girls, taking the piss out of other people etc.

'In terms of how it affected my exploration of gender and sex-uality, I wouldn't blame school entirely but it certainly retarded any exploration of either. At 14 I largely disengaged from people at school socially, became extremely religious and negative about sex – thought it was sinful etc. I became depressed and anxious and just funnelled all my energies into academic per-formance. It alleviated a bit as we got older – 17 and 18 – but I didn't consider sex or gender until I was 20, several years into university – I arrived at university saying I was asexual.

'The key thing being at an all-male school taught me was how to deploy humour as a defence mechanism. I was taunted as a "faggot", or whatever, every single day from age 12 to 15 but I hardened to this, and because I was sharp-witted I learned to retaliate and also to head it off before it began by being sarcastic or whatever first. I learned that in laddy male groups, humour goes a long way to currying favour and respect ("banter" as they like to call it) and I can still do this now if I find myself in an all-male group of straight guys – it's not my ideal social set up but it doesn't intimidate or faze me. That's what an all-boys school gave me. A lack of intimidation by men. If I had been in a mixed environment I believe I would have hidden myself in female friendship groups and still be anxious about lads to this day.'

Séan went on to work in finance – a career choice that may raise a few eyebrows, because of its reputation as being a hyper-masculine environment – but has since left to pursue writing. I asked them what this kind of career was like for someone such as themselves, and whether they felt under pressure to conform against their will.

'I worked in law, which is slightly less macho than hardcore banking and finance – it's more old boys' clubbish. Very softly spoken old-school men in suits – though some partners and clients were very gruff. Some of my clients were financiers who had amassed gargantuan fortunes and definitely saw the world as full of their bitches and steamrollered their way over that. I felt pressured to act "professional" – which is what you're told you must do. However, being professional is extremely gendered. It's a code of behaviour and presentation designed by men for men – it was obviously adapted for women when they began to feature more in professional firms, but they were still working with a male model. So yes – I did. I was disciplined for looking unprofessional at work twice – in reference to my hair being too long – and had to have it cut which I found hugely distressing and bizarrely made me realise how important my gender expression was to me. So there were indirect pressures – no one says "be more masculine" they say "you need to do this" and that thing is something associated with masculinity – like have short hair, wear a suit, talk to the client a certain way, talk to male partners in a certain register etc.'

Séan's story demonstrates how everyday attitudes and expectations towards masculinity affect LGBT people, but it can get a lot more serious than this too. A few chapters ago I wrote about Christina Bentley, a young trans woman serving in the Royal Air Force. Christina's story is one of the more positive of its kind, but it highlights quite how powerful our ideas of masculinity can be. She was able to come to terms with who she was, but sadly many trans people go through their lives unable to ever be themselves. Why? Because we constantly reinforce the idea that someone has to act in a certain way based entirely on the kind of genitals they have, and any refusal to do so can lead to verbal and physical abuse, and all too frequently, even murder. The insecurities of the male ego at its extreme are nothing short of deadly.

Trans women are significantly more likely to be murdered than the general population, and while there's no one reason for this shocking disparity, there have been a number of such incidents (particularly in the US) in recent years that share a depressing number of similarities: straight, cis men catcall or sexually harass women in public, and then, realising that the woman is transgender and presumably feeling ashamed or humiliated, they physically attack her. It seems that in these cases, the attackers' initial attraction to someone who turned out to be trans made them feel as if their sexuality was being challenged, and their response is to try to reclaim their masculinity by reacting violently. One of the defining qualities we tend to associate with masculinity is strength, but you will never see a greater display of weakness than when a man feels his masculinity is under fire.

MAN ARRESTED IN BRUTAL BEATING DEATH OF TRANSGENDER WOMAN

New York Post, 3rd March 2015[31]

A suspect has been arrested in the vicious beating death of a transgender woman in Harlem a year and a half ago, law enforcement sources said.

James Dixon, 24, was taken into custody and indicted Tuesday for the killing of Islan Nettles, 21.

Nettles was walking near the corner of Frederick Douglas Boulevard and West 148th Street on Aug. 17, 2013, when a man cat-called her and then became irate when he realized the object of his attention was transgender, police sources said.

Dixon punched Nettles in the face and head, knocking her unconscious, police said.

Nettles died five days later at Harlem Hospital, authorities said.

Toxic masculinity puts LGBT people at risk every day. As Laverne Cox, a trans actress known for her role in *Orange Is The New Black* said[32]: 'Just *being* trans out on the street is cause for our lives to be in danger.' But the problems are a lot more wide-ranging than that, and can both hurt LGBT people and turn them against others in the community. I've said at several points that toxic masculinity is largely a cishet male problem, but it's also evident in cis gay men, for pretty understandable reasons.

'It is internalised homophobia,' Séan Faye says. 'Yes, all men – especially when growing up – inculcate this fear of being perceived as gay. Gay men grow up with this too – hearing what they, in fact, are, is something to be ashamed of. Straight people probably assume that "coming out" (a process which straight people themselves create the need for by making themselves the default) is the end of all of this for a gay man. In fact, it is only the beginning. Often, coming out is the realisation that he cannot resist this categorisation anymore. It does not, necessarily, mean he is happy with it. Similarly, coming out leads the gay man into a new conceptual arena: one full of definitions of what it is to be a gay man that are largely speculative. Much of hetero-sexual culture – parents, schools, film and TV – will only give very brief clues and so I think a lot of gay men are struggling to see how much of these clues they take on board about how to live as "a gay man" and what the significance of gayness is.'

In the age we live in, it seems to be the case that a lot of straight liberals – myself included – like to believe that ours is a progressive society, and consider ourselves very supportive of LGBT rights because 'they're just like us'. This isn't necessarily helpful though, because in spite of our purportedly pro-queer stance, much of this sort of rhetoric only serves to reinforce antiquated traditions and values. Equal marriage, for example, was only a victory for gay people who wanted to conform with an old heterosexual tradition – and had the support of a number of conservatives for this very reason. This kind of support tends to exclude non-traditional ideas of love and sex, and in turn, this can cause a lot of gay men to react with expressions of toxic masculinity- because they know they'll only achieve mainstream acceptance if they act like straight men.

The gender binary we have traditionally subscribed to dictates a set of rules we must adhere to depending on the sex organs with which we were born. There's slightly more openness to definitions of gender than there used to be, but things haven't changed all that much. Masculinity, in particular, remains extremely rigid – as I said before, there's no positive equivalent to 'tomboy' for men who display effeminate characteristics, for example. Not only does this affect the way men behave, it shapes their attitudes to everyone around them. Since men have to conform so strictly, they can grow to resent any non-conformists, and this can manifest itself in a way that harms anyone who's not a cis straight man. And this doesn't just mean gay men and LGBT people – women of all sexualities and, particularly, feminists are hit hard by these ideals.

There are many different kinds of feminism, and many different schools of thought regarding what feminism's key objectives should be and what methods should be employed in achieving them. But at its most basic, feminism is a movement which strives for equality. It's about women having the same freedoms and privileges, and being able to do anything men can do.

I've brought up Men's Rights Activists (MRAs) a couple of times already in the book, but it's worth taking a quick look at them again now. The problem with MRAs is that they're focused less on helping men than harming women. James S. Fell, writing in *TIME*[33], said:

> Wait, what? *Men's* rights? That's a thing? Yes, it's a thing, and while there are certain legitimate aspects to men's rights activism, or MRA, it's overwhelmingly a toxic slew of misogyny. This world of resentment and hate speech has been brought to light in recent days as we learned about the vitriolic forum posts and videos left behind by Elliot Rodger, the 22 year-old accused of killing six people in Santa Barbara last week. But it's hard to comprehend from Rodger's delusional rants how potent the movement's message can be for ordinary men.
>
> MRAs believe the traditionally oppressed groups have somehow seized control and taken away their white male privilege. They tap into fear and insecurity and turn it into blame and rage. Often the leaders of these groups are men who feel as though they got screwed in a divorce. They quote all sorts of statistics about child custody and unfair alimony payments, because in their minds, the single mother who has to choose between feeding the kids or paying the rent is a myth. They believe passionately in their own victimhood and their creed goes something like this: *Women are trying to keep us down, usurp all our power, taking away what it means to be a man.*
>
> One popular MRA site is AVoiceForMen.com, with a mission to "expose misandry on all levels in our culture"

and "denounce the institution of marriage as unsafe and unsuitable for modern men" as well as "promote an end to chivalry in any form or fashion" and "educate men and boys about the threats they face in feminist governance." They also want an "end to rape hysteria" and promote "civil disobedience." In their defense, AVFM does support non-violence, but with all the inflammatory rhetoric, do readers always take heed?

There are Reddit threads and other Internet forums dedicated to men's rights, and the language and vitriol towards women and especially towards feminism is appalling. Any messages of nonviolence seem lost in the hate-mongering. These groups spew logically faulty statistics about the prevalence of male rape and spousal abuse, and how there really is no glass ceiling or pay inequality, and general complaints about how "that bitch got my promotion because she has a uterus."

One of the 'solutions' I've seen posited by MRAs in online discussions time and time again is a return to our old gender roles: they believe that the 'crisis of masculinity' has come about from women taking on traditionally masculine roles (i.e. having careers) which has left men feeling helpless and emasculated. However, the militant approach taken by these kinds of men is so repulsive to the general population, that not only is their aggression harmful to women, it's also backfired on them quite spectacularly: damaging the legitimate causes they claim to stand for and bringing down other, more reasonable men with them. Kate Harding wrote in *Jezebel*[34] of the movement:

Fuck you, first of all, for making it nearly impossible for decent men struggling with abusive partners or unfair custody arrangements to get the help they need and deserve. You have forever tainted those issues with your rage-filled, obsessively anti-woman horseshit, to the point where it's become difficult for any rational, compassionate person to trust a man who claims he's been screwed over in family court or abused by a female partner, even if he has.

That's right—I fully understand that those things happen. I fully believe that men in those situations deserve help, and I know they're generally less likely to ask for it than women are, not to mention less likely to find help there for them when they do go looking. I get how our society's ridiculously rigid ideas about masculinity mean that men are brought up to believe needing help will make them look weak, especially if it's a woman who's terrorizing them. I know those same suffocating standards also encourage men to stifle strong feelings and any nurturing tendencies, which deprives them of the right to experience the full range of human emotions without shame. That completely fucking sucks! You know how I know all that, and why I think it sucks?

BECAUSE I'M A FEMINIST.

Feminists are easily the biggest victims of MRAs: you'd struggle to find a feminist of any prominence who hasn't suffered harassment at their hands. Indeed, if you're a woman who writes or speaks on feminist issues at all in 2016, you face trolling and abuse online daily – hell, you face trolling and abuse online daily just for *existing* as a woman. But Harding highlights the hypocritical nature of Men's Rights, and the way its anti-feminist agenda actually causes destruction of its own kind. That's the thing with toxic masculinity: even when the direct victims of this behaviour are not cisgender, heterosexual men, it finds its way back to us.

Returning for a moment to the LGBT community, toxic masculinity creates a hierarchy within this which assigns privilege to cis men above all others *in exactly the same way as the rest of society.* Some cis gay guys, desperate to be higher up the social-standing ladder react to this (not necessarily consciously) just like their straight counterparts, by attempting to appear more masculine. This establishes their dominance within LGBT circles, and sees them getting a much easier ride at the expense of cis lesbians and trans or non-binary people. So not only do those groups face discrimination and bigotry by straight people, they're also hurt by gays – and again, like Séan said, it's not necessarily their fault, they are just playing the same game as the rest of us.

'Passing' is a word that is sometimes used to describe people who look the way society deems acceptable for someone of their gender. Trans people who 'pass' enjoy much more privilege than those who don't, essentially because they blend in with the people we've culturally decided are 'normal' – and this alone means they are less susceptible to the random abuse or attacks that visibly trans people routinely suffer. To some extent, 'passing' can also refer to cis gay people whose behaviour is an echo of how we generally consider straight people to behave. For gay men this means eschewing the effeminate or 'camp' mannerisms with which they're stereotypically associated and acting more 'masculine' – but just like the straight men who try so hard to conform with a stereotype, it rarely ends well. Perhaps the most vocally homophobic person I ever met was an enormous, shaven-headed Welsh raver named Lewis. He was openly gay, but after a few lagers would regularly yell in public: 'I fucking HATE queers!' He detested 'gay culture' and was very much opposed to setting foot inside gay bars and clubs, and while it was awkward having to explain to anyone who overheard his rants that 'It's okay, he's actually gay!' I understood where his frustration was coming from – he didn't want to be stereotyped or, specifically, thought of as different to the rest of us. And who could blame him? Even in our enlightened 21st-century world, LGBT people face so much othering and prejudice that anything a gay man can do to avoid being labelled by his sexuality is surely going to be tempting.

Unfortunately, it's also going to have a knock-on effect. As well as hurting other LGBT people, this form of toxic masculinity – like any – tends ultimately to lead to attacks on women, regardless of the men's sexuality. For a long time, gay men were mostly ignored or excused in discussions of misogyny, but what we've become more aware of is that certain gay men, though themselves persecuted, have taken advantage of their male privilege at the expense of women. It's not entirely their fault, though, much of the blame can be attributed to a society that prizes masculinity above all else.

Consequently, a handful of gay men have even become active in the Men's Rights community, something which MRAs have taken advantage of as proof of their cause being progressive and non-discriminatory. One gay man in particular – Milo Yiannopoulous, a journalist for the extreme right-wing website Breitbart – has become a figurehead for MRAs, and was notably involved in the GamerGate 'movement' – perhaps better described as a campaign of harassment which sought to bring down prominent female figures in the gaming industry over what it claimed was unethical media coverage in reviews*. I'm loathe to mention his name and give him any attention, because that's exactly what he craves; his contrarian opinions are cooked up solely to create controversy and offence. Yiannopoulous has supported attacks on numerous feminists, hiding behind his sexuality as if it excuses his behaviour. LGBT people are not just capable of finding themselves the victims of toxic masculinity, they can be so deeply affected by our entrenched ideas of gender that they end up continuing the cycle. It's testament to the incredible power of so-called masculinity that rather than allowing its victims to team up and fight the real problem, it manages to divide and turn one group against others. Arguably it's because of our obsession with masculinity – and by consequence our continued insistence on viewing gender as a firm binary and not a wide spectrum – that infighting has become rampant even in feminist circles.

Toxic masculinity, the patriarchy, gender roles, and everything that makes this triumvirate possible are the biggest threats to both LGBT people and women. Every group that's

---

* Zoe Quinn, a games developer and one of the women targeted, was falsely accused of entering into a relationship with a gaming journalist in exchange for positive coverage of games she had developed. Similar accusations were aimed at other women attacked as part of this controversy.

been marginalised on account of gender and sexuality has a common enemy, yet ends up fighting the others rather than joining forces to defeat the true evil.

For those of us at the top of the social hierarchy – i.e. me and my fellow straight white men: hi! – it might be tempting to sit back and watch the chaos ensue, but we mustn't do this – for their sake, of course, but also for ours.

Society views straight as the default for both women and men, but because of the perceived power of masculinity and male superiority over women, the default for men has a far bigger impact on the bigger picture. Whether or not it's a conscious decision, we're essentially saying that anything other than straight is bad, and this fucks up a lot of people. It's responsible for a good deal of the toxic masculinity we see in both straight and gay men, as well as the hierarchy within the LGBT community I mentioned earlier. It's not enough just to support equal marriage and think 'oh isn't it lovely that they can be just like us' – all that this does is to give a select few gay people the chance to conform with our old traditions while anyone who's not a monogamous cisgender person gets left behind. That's not LGBT equality – it's letting gay people whose lifestyles conform to a straight stereotype achieve legal and social parity. It's merely the *acceptable* face of homosexuality. What this tells boys and young men is that *being* gay is okay, but *acting* it – or rather, acting in the camp unmasculine manner society deems to be an inherent characteristic of homosexuality – is not. Until this changes, toxic masculinity motivated by homophobia will remain as powerful as ever – and may even get worse in gay men. Such is the power of the patriarchy, that a group whose actions were only decriminalised very recently have been able to ascend the ranks – arguably above women – because of their masculinity. It's a horrifying thought that women could start to face more opposition rather than less, for a wide variety of reasons (of which I'm obviously going to focus on the most selfish ones because I'm a man).

We need women.

And we need feminism. We need it to fight for real equality, and not just serve the needs of a select few like the Men's Rights movement does.

We need LGBT people too, and not just monogamous gay men. We need them to teach us we don't have to conform in order to be decent people. We need trans, non-binary, queer people to show us we needn't be bound by the gender assigned to us, that it's okay to let ourselves go and not push our masculinity at every opportunity. A society in which women and queer people are given no input is a brutal, grey and lifeless one in which I suspect even the most hard-line conservatives would hate to live.

I don't mean they owe it to us to be our educators and pick up after our shitty selves, but that we can learn from them just through their presence in our lives. We owe it to them. Masculinity has, for humanity's entire existence, dictated the way that everyone's life should be lived. Now this has to change.

Toxic masculinity is entirely self-serving, it brings no benefit beyond boosting our own egos and staving off insecurities. It is a false, hollow and cheap representation of masculinity, which is wrecking our lives and those of everyone around us. Worst of all, it ruins the lives of people who are not merely bystanders;

they are the people who can actually help fix us up and rid us of the damage we can do to ourselves. If we could learn to accept – not just accept, actively celebrate – all LGBT people, and not just those who act like us, there would be no default sexuality or gender identity, because we would actually see them as equals. There would be no need to fear how anyone perceived our sexuality, because it wouldn't make any difference to how we were treated, so we wouldn't have to act like anyone else. True LGBT equality could have a profound effect on toxic masculinity.

It's the same case with how we treat women. Let's put aside for a moment the benefits that we reap from women, providing vital emotional support and so on, and look at the bigger picture. Toxic masculinity is bred, at its most basic, by a fear of emasculation. Emasculation is considered perhaps the worst thing that could happen to a man, so much so that we will risk death in order to avoid it. There's no real equivalent of emasculation for women. Why? Because they're already at the bottom. Men fear emasculation possibly because it will bring them down to that level, make them equals of women – or perhaps less attractive *to* women. I realise that sounds incredibly melodramatic, and should add that I don't think it's a conscious thought many men have, but it really does come down to that. I saw it summed up quite neatly by a tweet, albeit in the context of race: 'Why are white people so scared of becoming a minority in the 2040s? Are minorities treated badly in America or something?'

There are myriad reasons why women and feminists are so important to us if we're to tackle toxic masculinity, though one in particular stands out. The number one goal of feminism is to achieve gender equality in every aspect of our lives, and while it's a long way off I'm hopeful it'll get there. And when it does, emasculation could arguably cease to exist. If men are no longer above women, we'll have nowhere to fall; no reason to fear being their equals if we already are. Not because we descended or lost anything, but because they climbed their way up. That's not to say masculinity and femininity will cease to exist, they will simply change, and adopt whatever values are necessary at that time.

If you're reading this, I'd say there's a pretty good chance you believe there are problems with masculinity. You might not agree that feminism or LGBT rights are the key to solving these problems, but I'd ask that you consider the following: if masculinity is indeed hurting men in a unique way, then it's proof that gender inequality exists. You can't solve inequality with further inequality, it doesn't work like that. You have to fight for the opposite. And if you're not willing to get behind gender and LGBT equality then toxic masculinity will continue to fuck with us all.

Losing It: Sex, Rape Culture, and the Frustration of Male Virginity

TEEN BOYS LOSING VIRGINITY EARLIER AND EARLIER,

REPORT TEEN BOYS

The Onion, 29th April 2014

Okay, maybe your fancy 'academic texts' written by 'experts' in 'gender studies' don't quote headlines from satirical news sites at the beginning of chapters, but you know what? Sometimes *The Onion* speaks more truth than all of the legitimate journals on Earth put together. Regardless of gender, adolescence can be a fucking *miserable* time; a cocktail of hormones, peer pressure and insecurity, all complemented by a virtually non-existent self-esteem. If there's one piece of advice I'd want to give anyone in the midst of this period, it would be 'don't trust anyone who tells you these are the best years of your life'.

In the last chapter, I discussed at length how perceived sexuality affects the ways we, as men, present ourselves, and the widespread fear that acting at all 'gay' or 'effeminate' will lead to us being targeted by bullies. We are taught that our sexuality is a major defining characteristic of our personalities long before puberty sets in, and then after this it just gets even more complicated – after all, so much of what we are forced to endure at this age is a direct result of our reaching sexual maturity. But in reality, this biological occurrence is made most unbearable by sociological factors (like the pedestal on which sex is placed) without which it would be much easier to handle the physical and chemical changes our bodies go through.

As a society, our obsession with sex is so powerful that even those who are able to look at it objectively and see that this obsession is ridiculous are still plagued by the same worries about the issue as everyone else. I was lucky to have a non-judgmental, supportive group of friends in my teens, who would never think less of each other for what sexual action they were or weren't getting; I didn't believe for one second that getting laid would actually make me any better as a person or that it mattered what age I was when I first had sex; I was fully aware that when it did happen it probably wouldn't be the mind-blowing, life-affirming act it's hyped up to be. In the rational part of my brain, I knew that sex wasn't everything, and even so, during that entire time, I wanted nothing more than to lose my virginity. (I'm conscious of the fact my mum is probably going to read this, hi Mum! Maybe skip the next couple of paragraphs, yeah?) I wasn't really fussed about who I lost it to or whether we had any kind of emotional connection, it came down almost entirely to the desire to have been inside a woman, just once, in order to get that experience out of the way. It wasn't even a matter of being able to brag about it, I simply craved the self-reassurance that would come with no longer being a virgin.

So it happened, and confirmed everything I already knew. Now I'm in my twenties and feel reasonably qualified to say: 'Sex is fun, but it's not necessarily going to be a life-changing experience or anywhere near important enough to spend time worrying about if you've yet to lose your virginity.' It's the truth, and most sexually active people would back me up on this, but reading it won't make the slightest difference to a desperate boy in his teens. No amount of others' wisdom or lived experience can change the fact that it's really, really frustrating when everyone around you seems to be gunning for a world record in Most Sex Had and you're stuck with just your imagination and one wrist that's suspiciously more toned than the other. Of course, it's not just males who struggle with sex (or the lack thereof), but while our desires and anxieties may be equally as strong, the cultures surrounding sexuality in young men and women, and the consequences, are quite different.

If you were to take two teenagers – one boy, one girl – with an otherwise identical background (socioeconomic status, school, academic performance, popularity etc), both of whom have slept with an above-average number of partners, which of the two would you guess had faced the most criticism or abuse for their sex life? If your answer was 'the boy', then – no offence or anything – my follow up question would be: where the *fuck* have you been all your life?

Male sexuality overwhelmingly tends to be celebrated, guys who shag lots of women are seen as being 'studs', and as something that other men aspire to be; women, on the other hand, are shamed for the same thing, called names such as 'slut' or 'whore', and taught that only pure, virgin women are desirable to men. This might have something to do with our historical ownership of women – by taking a man's hand in marriage, a woman was essentially agreeing to become his property; and men presumably didn't want what they perceived to be second-hand goods. To quote Laurie Penny: 'The ideal woman is fuckable, but never actually fucks.'[35] Even from a linguistic standpoint our sexism is all too apparent: every derogatory term for a promiscuous person is gendered, and in the rare instances that these words are used to refer to men, we tend to tack on a prefix, 'whore' becomes 'man-whore', and so on. I am sure that no one in the history of the English language has ever called anyone a 'woman-whore' – the prefix is unnecessary, and in its original form, 'whore' refers only to women.

The interplay of virginity and masculinity is also particularly interesting. While historically (albeit sometimes inaccurately) a broken hymen indicated a woman's lost virginity, there is no equivalent for men, and yet culturally male virginity seems to be somewhat more taboo, particularly among older people. Christ knows enough women have to deal with endless shaming for promiscuity, but there don't seem to be the same tropes surrounding older female virgins as there are for men.*

Everyone knows the character; the overweight, unemployed, 30-something guy who lives in his parents' basement and plays video games – a good example is Comic Book Guy from The Simpsons. The fact that he's a virgin is a detail that, like all the others, is intended to present him as a loser. Off the top of my head I'm unable to think of a notable example in pop

---

* You could argue 'spinster' is used as such, but I would suggest that's specific to marriage rather than virginity.

culture in which an older woman's virginity is seen as something embarrassing or shameful in quite the same way. That's not to say women don't suffer from the same insecurities about this as men, but as I discussed in the earlier chapter The Ideal Man, the way each is presented in society and deemed 'acceptable' or otherwise is quite different. Certain actions or comments, which would rightly be considered sexist in the modern world if made by men about women, are laughed off when the subject is male. Take a look at the following snippet taken from an interview with Michael Fassbender in *GQ*[36]:

> Let's consider a remarkable interview with him in *The Sunday Times*, a British newspaper known for a reasonably high tone and sturdy standards. Much of the article is about Fassbender's anatomy, sex life, and sexual history, and in the published version he is depicted as someone willingly engaged in the back-and-forth. At one point he is quoted as blurting out, unexpectedly, "When in doubt, fuck." It also includes a statement near the end from the interviewer, Camilla Long, that I believe is without precedent even in the giddy history of the celebrity profile:
>
> *I...feel quite certain that he would willingly show me his penis, given slightly different circumstances and a bucket of champagne.*
>
> "Wow," says Fassbender when I recite this to him. "No, I haven't read that one. Just as well, really." But he does remember the interview. "The first thing she said to me was, 'So, what does it feel like to have a big cock?' That was her opening question."

The way we talk about male sexuality is entirely different to the way we discuss female sexuality, to the extent that people who really should know better are guilty of this bizarre elevation of sexual prowess as long as it's about a man.

Historically, virginity has been prized in women. As I mentioned above, the unbroken hymen was symbolic of purity, proof that a woman hadn't been 'tainted' by another man before marriage and all a bit indicative of male possessiveness. We've mostly got past the idea that sex before marriage is immoral or impure, but it's still a common fantasy of plenty of men to take a woman's virginity (maybe because she won't know how bad he is at sex). Virgin men, however, don't tend to be subject to this same fetishisation, and instead can be seen as inexperienced and thus undesirable. I would hazard a guess that only a minority of men willingly admit to a woman that she's their first partner, at least not until the deed is done, fearing that the revelation will be a deal breaker. Men are frequently taught by their peers, their parents and much of society to believe that dominance – particularly over women – is a key quality of masculinity, and they worry that by admitting their virginity to a more experienced partner, she'll view them as weak or submissive. In fact, this may go some way to explaining why male virginity in general is viewed the way it is.

Being dominant and assertive plays into many aspects of society's ideas of male success, from high-paying careers to beautiful wives. When men have passed their twenties without losing their virginity, they're portrayed as 'sad' or 'losers': words that are surprisingly gendered, and that are rarely used in the same context to describe adult women.

Masculinity and a fairly rigid definition of 'success' are synonymous, and the concept of a personified human 'failure' on an
all-encompassing financial and personal scale is applied almost
exclusively to men. As I mentioned right at the beginning of the
book, modern perceptions of masculinity have been shaped in
a big way by the jobs we do, the money we earn and, above all,
how much *power* we command. Attitudes to romantic relationships or fatherhood have not – until very recently – been factored
into the value that society ascribes to men, while women have
traditionally been judged on these alone. Does she make a good
wife? Is she raising her kids properly? Male success is all about
power, and if a man is seen as powerful then rarely do we question his merits as a father or partner.

There's a word I've touched upon a few times already, but
which I feel is appropriate here: emasculation. In modern usage,
emasculation tends to refer to a loss of masculinity as a socialised concept, but it can also mean, quite literally, the removal
of the male genitalia. The evolution of the way the word has
been defined over time suggests we're burdened by a much
more complex idea of what it means to be a man than we used
to be, but its origins betray what we fear most at our core. A
man without genitals can function as a human in a way that a
man without a heart can not, but he is unable to have sex – and
so, by this definition, he is not a man. Perhaps this is why we
view male virginity as a bad thing – without having had sexual
intercourse, a man is not a man.

There are many reasons we want to have sex, but there's
no denying that for straight men in particular, a good sex life
(regular, satisfying, ideally with a variety of partners) is seen as

an important part of masculinity. As I touched upon earlier, loud heterosexuality is fundamental to the definition of masculinity to which many subscribe, so it's not surprising that we celebrate physical sexuality like this: a man having sex with a woman is literally the most heterosexual thing he can do (although I'm sure there's room here for a dated remark about Elton John having had a wife). Physical sexuality is linked to masculinity so powerfully that it may prove one of the hardest attitudes to change, held even by those who should know better. Male virginity and penis size are common punchlines, and I've been disappointed on several occasions to see these sorts of jokes made by otherwise intelligent, forward-thinking feminists, often in response to online harassment.

Like the Australian road safety campaign (chapter four)* I can understand the reasoning behind this – if you link misogyny to things men are ashamed about, it might make them think twice before tweeting abuse – but regardless of whether it's effective, it perpetuates the harmful idea that a man's worth is found in the size of his genitals or in his sex life. Imagine a well-meaning man who hasn't had sex for whatever reason, being forced to hear from someone he respects that another man's shitty personality is a result of him being a virgin. On a similar note, there are plenty of horrible men who have slept with countless women, and/or have massive dicks, and plenty

---

* In the latter part of last decade, a campaign in New South Wales featured images of women waving their pinkie fingers at young men who sped past, with the slogan 'Speeding: No One Thinks Big Of You'. The premise was clear and to the point: if you drive unsafely, people assume your penis is small. Based on available statistics, it was also a resounding success, drastically reducing the number of accidents year on year.

of wonderful men with more modest packages, and when you make comments like these, you risk alienating the good guys and further provoking the bad ones. This is what we're up against: men are being taught by people from across the spectrum that they are defined by their physical sexuality, and that being a virgin is something to be ashamed of. Girls may want sex, but boys are encouraged to believe they *need* it. And this is very dangerous indeed.

For as long as sex education in schools has existed, sex education in schools has been bad. I don't think I've ever met anyone, from any place, of any age, who thought their Sex Ed. classes – or class, singular, as is often the case – were time well spent. Grainy videos with animated erections being soundtracked, hilariously, by slide-whistles; naked fathers and sons walking towards the camera so you could see the difference between prepubescent and adult genitals (except the father was sporting an almost enviable hair coverage which all but obscured his scrotum); someone pointing to a table of contraceptives with little indication as to how any of them worked. If you were lucky you'd get to roll a condom onto a perfectly straight, plastic phallus, your teacher laughing nervously as the boys cheered the enthusiastic efforts of one of the girls. There was rarely any discussion of sex outside of a biological context, or any mention of why you probably shouldn't get pregnant yet, and we shall soon be approaching a third generation of kids failed by the same ancient VHS, doomed to repeat the mistakes of their parents and grandparents.

The content of these lessons is now more redundant than ever. Most kids are well-versed in the physical side of sex thanks to phones and the internet, with tabloid headlines proclaiming every few weeks the 'shocking number' of children who view porn regularly. Everyone's worried about what exposure to this material at so young an age is doing to our youth, but few are bothering to ask why a situation has arisen in which youths routinely seek out sexually explicit content, nor do they ask how we should address it. As far as I'm concerned, if someone is voluntarily seeking out porn and enjoying it, they've obviously reached an age of sexual awareness and it's not the end of the world. For some kids, this may be spawned by an initial curiosity, a result of insufficient sex education; for others, their reasons for watching porn will be exactly the same as those of any adult. Porn in and of itself is not necessarily unhealthy. However, problems can begin to appear when it's being consumed by young people as their first real experience of sex, and their minds can be unable to distinguish porn from the real thing.

This, in turn, means that when they start becoming sexually active, their behaviour may reflect what they've seen in porn and this can be harmful for themselves and their partners on an emotional level, they can leave partners feeling degraded or used, but it can also have physical effects, as porn rarely shows the discussion or consent vital in real life and in some cases could be considered to be normalising risky practices. Acts such as anal sex are ubiquitous in porn, and while plenty of real life couples can enjoy this, it requires total enthusiasm from both parties and a lot of preparation – a young man trying to emulate the unlubricated anal sex he's seen time and time again can do serious damage to his partner's body.

Emily Reynolds, a journalist who's written on mental health

and feminism told me: 'I don't think I've ever been with a man who doesn't watch porn, but within that group the vast majority have been able to separate the fantasy of porn from their real life interactions with, and attitudes to, women. In my experience most men are fully aware of the fact porn is a complete artifice – a lot of young men have sexual tastes that may have been implicitly *influenced* by porn, but in a manner that doesn't necessarily affect the way they treat women in general (although there is a lot to unpick around why people may like certain things and how pornography has consciously or subconsciously influenced that). I had one boyfriend, though, who was absolutely *obsessed* with porn.'

She once asked him to give up watching porn – not out of any kind of moral objection but as a test. 'He absolutely lost it. It was like I'd asked him to give up food for a week or something – he just couldn't not watch it.' Reynolds believes her ex-boyfriend's obsession with porn was part of a bigger issue 'in that he didn't respect women and he wanted to control them.

'Unable to do that in real life, he really took solace in watching porn because it was ten perfect minutes of ultimate control. As a viewer he was controlling them because he was the client, the customer; in his mind, and in that moment, he was the singular voyeur and audience for whatever particular act the woman was performing. And, unlike me, they always said yes – the whole point of (most) porn is that women are constantly assenting, they're either wordlessly accepting or loudly encouraging the scene. That was something that I could never do because, obviously, I'm a real life human woman with different desires and bad moods and my own autonomy. I couldn't always say yes and he resented that.'

Though I am no fan of Martin Daubney, the former editor of lads' mag *Loaded*, I do agree with his stance on teaching young men the responsible way to consume porn. As he wrote in the *Guardian*[37]:

My take on porn is like my take on alcohol: prohibition will always fail, but it's similarly risky to hand kids the keys to the drinks cabinet. Instead, we need to encourage responsible and critical consumption – and those conversations need to happen in schools and at home.

With porn, I urge teenagers to question what they see, rather than accepting it as true. Not all men have penises like draught excluders. You don't have to shave yourself bald: not everybody likes it like that. If you see something in porn and you want to try it in the real world – always ask first. And if the person says no, then no always means no.

When I was seven, my dad pointed out battered women we'd occasionally see on the streets of Nottingham, where I grew up, and say: "We don't do it like that, son. Real men don't do it like that." Now I try to take perhaps the most uncomfortable stimulus of our time into British schools and turn it into a positive springboard for a 21st-century conversation about sex and consent. The kids, and especially the lads, listen to me, as my perhaps dubious CV gives me credibility. They know I won't judge them and, vitally, I'm not there the next day to make them feel uncomfortable.

This is when the real conversations start – with teachers, their parents, and, hopefully, the most importantly people of all: their future sexual partners.

I don't think young people watching porn is inherently bad, but there are definitely issues to be addressed – such as the aforementioned blurring of fantasy and reality, consent, respect for one's partner and general bedroom etiquette – and this is where sex education could make such an important difference. It is undeniable that today children find out more about the physical side of sex from other sources than they ever learn in school, and much earlier too, so while the basics should still be covered (not every child has access to such information), a much-needed update and shift in direction could leave kids walking out of their Sex Ed. classes having actually learned something useful, beyond the surprising amount of water a condom can hold before it bursts.

In the last few years, campaigners have been calling on the government and schools to broaden the discussion that takes place in Sex Ed. classes, emphasising areas such as emotional development and relationships, and most notably the issue of consent. It's a topic that's vitally important and so simple to understand, that the fact it's largely ignored is genuinely troubling. Part of the problem may stem from the fact that consent is seen as something unambiguous, so we assume there is no need to talk about it. But this couldn't be further from the truth.

In December 2015, British journalist Emma Garland wrote a stunning (albeit uncomfortable to read) piece entitled 'Defining absence'[38]. Prompted by allegations made against the porn actor James Deen by his former partner Stoya (herself a porn actress), Garland described her own experience of being raped by a close friend, and her subsequent difficulty in accepting, on a personal level, that she had been sexually assaulted – because it didn't fit in with the definition society generally assigns to rape:

No matter how many times we hear it, we're always surprised when we're faced with a case of rape taking place within a relationship. It doesn't fit the framework of the stereotypical narrative – a dark alley, a stranger in a balaclava, a police report – and so it's either questioned heavily or rejected completely. In reality though, of the 85,000 women and 12,000 men raped in England and Wales every year approximately 90% know the person who did it. So the real question here isn't why should we believe these women, but rather, why shouldn't we? Not everybody is able to talk about their abuse straight away, or publicly, or even at all. It isn't always immediately obvious to people that sexual abuse has happened, or is happening, to them. It took over two years for me to recognise my own.

A couple of months before she wrote this, a picture of a student at Warwick University went viral. The young man in the picture, George Lawlor, was holding up a sign that read 'THIS IS NOT WHAT A RAPIST LOOKS LIKE' in response to his having being invited to an event that centred on teaching consent and dispelling myths about sexual violence. Self-awareness, amongst other things, is clearly not Lawlor's strongpoint. As Garland said, popular portrayals of rapists paint them as sub-human creatures, disturbed loners who strike under the cover of darkness. They are deplored by society, and rightly so, for their crime is horrendous. In reality, though, the crime of rape is more often than not committed by perfectly normal looking, charming, charismatic, well-liked men, whose victims are known to them and whose crimes often go unreported. Rapists, in actual fact, frequently do look like the well-dressed, middle-class, university-educated people with whom George Lawlor identifies – they're not all wearing the exact shirt/sweater combination you'd expect of the communications secretary for a university's Conservative Association, but it's damn well close enough. If you've ever read about how rape destroys victims' lives, and found yourself asking how the attacker can live with himself knowing the pain and trauma for which he's responsible, then by the end of the next sentence you will understand why we need to start teaching boys about consent.

Many rapists don't know that they're rapists.

Before I go any further, I want to take a moment to define a term I'll be using a fair bit in this chapter: rape culture. According to Emilie Buchwald in her book *Transforming a Rape Culture*: 'Rape culture is a complex of beliefs that encourages male sexual aggression and supports violence against women. It occurs in a society where violence is seen as sexy and sexuality as violent. In a rape culture women perceive a continuum of threatened violence that ranges from sexual remarks to sexual touching to rape itself. A rape culture condones physical and emotional terrorism against women as the norm. In a rape culture both men and women assume that sexual violence is a fact of life, inevitable as death or taxes. This violence, however, is neither biologically nor divinely ordained. Much of what we accept as inevitable is in fact the expression of values and attitudes that can change.'[39]

Beyond Buchwald's definition, rape culture is the practice of trivialising, mocking or joking about sexual assault, it describes a society that blames rape victims while protecting the actual rapists, or skates over the issue to the extent that many young people don't even understand what constitutes rape. It's true that our understanding of what rape is has changed vastly over the last half-century: today there are still many countries in the world whose legal systems don't accept that rape can exist within marriage, and for a very long time in British culture (and this is something that has only recently begun to change) rape was seen in the very narrow definition of occurring only at the hands of an anonymous attacker abducting the victim in a public place.

Over the last two or three years, college campuses in the United States have become notorious hotspots for sex offences, with the outcry over the tolerance of rape culture and the attendant reluctance of universities to punish those responsible for the crimes making international headlines. A study published at the end of 2014 gave a fairly powerful insight into a major cause of the epidemic, citing the results of a survey that showed 32% of men at American colleges would have 'intentions to force a woman to sexual intercourse' if 'nobody would ever know and there wouldn't be any consequences'[40]. When the question was rephrased to include the word 'rape', this number dropped to 13.6%. Although this is still *disturbingly* high, the disparity between the two sets of results does at least suggest a lot of college students simply don't know what rape is.

'No means no' was for a long time a well-known slogan of anti-rape campaigns, its message clear and concise: if you have sex with a woman after she has said she doesn't want you to, it's rape. This remains the definition of rape in many people's minds, but it has begun to fall out of favour due to its being legally incorrect (the absence of consent can now be just as damning in court as an explicit refusal) and the way in which it implicitly places the blame for the rape on the victim if they didn't explicitly say no. Advocacy groups such as Campaign4Consent are now calling for young men to be taught that consent must be given actively, rather than assumed passively, and furthermore that it must be delivered with enthusiasm. All too often, men have justified their actions – both to themselves and in legal settings – by saying the victim didn't explicitly say no, despite the victim often being too intoxicated to know what was happening. This requirement of enthusiastic consent is vitally important if we are to address rape culture, not only to reduce the crime rate itself, but to ensure that the perpetrators are properly dealt with and justice is served. A friend recently confided in me that several years ago she was the victim of an attempted rape by a taxi driver. When she went to the police to report the incident the first thing they asked was whether she had led him on in any way – a familiar story to thousands of victims, and just one reason of many why better education is crucial.

Returning to Emma Garland's piece, we can see how even in situations where the victim has clearly said no, they can be left questioning the complexities of the attack and still be reluctant to report it:

It was late, everyone was asleep in their separate rooms in the apartment we were sharing, and I was miserable. My best friend was rooming with her boyfriend, so I text who I felt was the next closest person to me at that time asking if he was awake and could I please come and sit in his room and quietly not die. "Of course," he said. I went in and lay down next to him in his bed and cried into his armpit while he hugged me, trying to console me—a pose we had found ourselves holding so many times before. At different stages in our lives I had gone to him for comfort and I had gone to him for sex, but the two were never part and parcel. It was strictly one or the other. That night, I went to him for comfort, crying and shaking and wondering if I'd even make it to the end of the trip.

I was still crying when he started kissing me and, even though I wasn't in a mind to even consider wanting to, I kissed him back out of habit. It started to go further. I said "don't". He continued, I said "no". I said "no" more than once. I was still crying. He started having sex with me and I tried to push him off, but he carried on anyway. I guess at some point I realised he was planning to carry on until he was done, so I did all the things I had to do to make it end faster. When he finished, he immediately asked me to leave the room because he had a girlfriend (not present) and it would look bad if anyone realised I had slept there. I wandered around the apartment for a while in the dark, not feeling depressed or upset—but something nameless defined by the total absence of feeling. I distracted myself by Facebook messaging in-jokes to my internet crush. I did that until I fell asleep and never brought it up again.

Because of how it happened and who had done it, I shied away from calling it rape. The absence of physical struggle coupled with the fact that I had pursued it in the past made me believe that I must have consented even though I felt certain I hadn't. I carried the weight of it around with me for years, never saying anything, never fully connecting it to the feelings of worthlessness that were there anyway because of the depression but somehow confirmed by his actions. I spent years weighing up my emotional and mental health against his consequences, trying to quantify whether it was worth saying anything, or whether there was even anything to say. In retrospect that entire period of my life has all the trademarks of a manic episode: decreased sleep, financial recklessness (I was approximately £2,000 in credit card debt), impulsive decision-making, sexual frivolousness in general, wild academic ambitions, and feeling so confident that I had a handle on all of the above that any negative consequences must have been my own design. Had I had just remembered it incorrectly? Had I not been as clear as I thought in my opposition? There was also the impossible task of explaining what happened to our mutual friends and hoping they would believe me. And even if they did, then what? Overwhelmed, I said nothing. I considered myself lucky that it hadn't been violent. I considered myself lucky that it didn't have any long or short-term effects on my sexual health or relationships. I considered myself lucky that I didn't get pregnant, and that if I had then at least I lived in a country where I would be able to terminate it if I chose to. The only thing I didn't consider was myself.

Back in chapter two I wrote about how, for most of history, women's biology dictated that they had to be the primary child-carer, and how in spite of technological advancements that have made this no longer the case, we have created a socio-logical issue reflective of that once inevitable aspect of biology, and consequently women continue to face discrimination for absolutely no logical reason. The act of sexual intercourse is a similar illustration of how taking a once solely biological instinct and allowing it to define gender in sociological terms is point-lessly damaging.

Men have always held the power when it comes to sex. At a primal level, the structure of their sex organs allowed early men to inseminate women (and thus continue their family tree) regardless of the women's willingness, whereas the require-ment for male arousal (i.e. an erection) to reproduce means that women are unable to force conception in the way men can. Historically, if they wanted to bear children, women would have first had to attract a mate. It has long been assumed that the biological reason that features such as large breasts and thighs on women are considered attractive is because they were indicative of a woman's ability to bear and feed children, and a preference for these features remains a part of our instincts.

Most of the sex we have today – at least in more secular, developed countries – is not for the purposes of reproduction; widely-available contraception has allowed us to bypass its pri-mary biological purpose and we do it, essentially, because it feels really good – the initial reasons for which, we can only assume, were to motivate us to have lots of sex in the first place. Sometimes we do still do it to make babies, and it can strengthen the bond in a romantic relationship, but mostly we have sex because it might feel good for a short time. Obviously this is great, but it does beg the question of why sex is spoken about these days as if it were the be-all and end-all of humanity. If it was *that* good, why did we bother inventing civilisation instead of just spending the last 10,000 years having an orgy in a cave?

Furthermore, there are plenty of other things we take extreme pleasure from that aren't elevated to the same status as sex. I'm reminded of Renton's description of what heroin feels like in *Trainspotting*: 'Take the best orgasm you ever had, multiply it by a thousand and you're still nowhere near it.' The thing is, absurd though our obsession may be, none of this would really be an issue if it was just about enjoying sex. It's when you start drawing links between sex and personal worth that problems start to arise.

The power early men wielded solely because of their penises is still strong today. Arguably, rape is often less an act of sexual desire than one of power and dominance, which is why it has been used en masse in war-torn countries as a means of oppression. It is probably the last remaining way men can exert their power over women in a purely biological sense: misogyny at its most basic. But now consider the way that we, as a society, equate a man's power with his penis size and sexual ability. By perpetuating the outdated idea that a man's biology is directly linked to his personality, we are ignoring the fact that for all of history, the only way a penis has really been powerful is as a weapon used against women.

Even after we abandoned our hunter-gatherer lives and moved towards a more civilised world, biology was used by men against women. The role of women as child bearers and the consequent workplace domination by men meant women were slaves to men, financially and sexually, because they were unable to support themselves. Now, with men able to care for children and contraception giving women autonomy over their own bodies, we are nearly independent of the biological aspects of gender that allowed men to oppress women for so long. Rape is the last remaining weapon of a man's biological sex that he can use against women. Telling a man his worth resides in his penis does nothing more than sociologically reinforce what are now all-but redundant biological aspects of gender that were used against women for all of human history – which is why I find it so surprising to see feminists make jokes about the size of a guy's dick.

Some men can be consumed by their insecurities on this matter, allowing those insecurities to shape their behaviour in horrific ways. In early 2015, teenager Ben Moynihan was convicted of the attempted murders of three women. The attacks, he said, were in revenge for the fact he was still a virgin. All of his victims were strangers, but he chose them solely because they were women, fuelled by his desire to punish *any* woman, because he had been hurt by others. It echoed the case of Eliot Rodger, who killed six people in Isla Vista, California in 2014, his bloodthirst born from an anger towards women who had rejected him, and men who enjoyed a more sexually active life than his own. *The Independent* reported[41]:

Moynihan, who called himself the "unhappy geezer", left letters for police confessing to his crimes in the run-up to his arrest. In one, left on a police van, he taunted officers for not apprehending him and wrote: "All women needs [sic] to die and hopefully next time I can gouge their eyeballs out."

In another, he wrote: "Every time I stab someone I run home and I like to smell the flesh I ripped out". He concluded the letter by telling police to come and arrest him before he hurt anyone else.

In a video found on his laptop, Moynihan filmed himself describing his frustration at being unable to lose his virginity, saying: "I think every girl is a type of slut, they are fussy with men nowadays, they do not give boys like us a chance.

I am still a virgin, everyone is losing it before me, that's why you are my chosen target. I just can't live in this flat, I have no future here. So women, tell me how we should do this."

The violence was an extreme reaction to misogynistic beliefs that are all too common. When men are taught to value sex – particularly for the first time – above all else, it can breed a sense of entitlement and a belief that women owe them something: an attitude that, ironically, tends to backfire. After repeated failed conquests, rather than considering that they themselves might be responsible, men can begin to harbour feelings of betrayal, mistrust and hatred towards women which, over time, they then try to legitimise and justify. Although few would admit it, the fact is that a lot of misogyny can be traced back to a man's sexual advances being rejected. These attitudes are particularly prevalent among Men's Rights Activists (MRAs), a group broadly defined by their mistrust of feminism, support of traditional gender roles and criticism of the way men are supposedly demonised in society and discriminated against. Much has been written about MRAs over the last couple of years, although one recent feature in *The Sunday Times*[42] (again by Martin Daubney) stood out, opening:

> David Sherratt, 18, is a chemistry student at Cardiff University. He has never had a girlfriend and isn't planning on finding one. Not now. Not ever.
>
> "Hook-up sex is too risky for words," he says. "Girls can wake up the next day and claim you raped them. I'm genuinely too scared to go near a woman — just in case. At university, I'm made to feel like a rapist all the time... I've never had a relationship and I don't think that's going to happen anytime soon. It's just too dangerous."

False rape accusations are very serious, and can destroy the life of someone who has been wrongly accused. Even when the accused has been cleared of any charges, the damage may already have been done, which has led to some people calling for suspects in rape cases to be granted – until proven guilty – the same anonymity offered to victims. In the wake of the Jimmy Savile revelations, in which many of his victims said that they had felt unable to report the crimes until others had done so publicly, it seems unlikely this will happen any time soon for fear of preventing victims coming forward. Whatever happens, false rape accusations are immensely harmful. But they're also incredibly rare, and we have to remember this for the sake of rape victims. From the *Guardian*[43], in 2013:

> A "misplaced belief" that false accusations of rape or domestic violence are commonplace may be undermining

police and prosecutors' efforts to investigate such crimes, the director of public prosecutions has warned.

The study released [...] by the Crown Prosecution Service (CPS) reveals that during the 17-month test period – when all false allegation cases were referred to the DPP – there were 5,651 prosecutions for rape and 111,891 for domestic violence in England and Wales.

By comparison, over the same timespan, there were only 35 prosecutions for making false allegations of rape, six for false allegations of domestic violence and three that involved false allegations of both rape and domestic violence.

It seems that for young men like the aforementioned David Sherratt, their fear of being falsely accused of rape comes not from an increase in false rape accusations, but from a culture that's beginning to talk about sexual assault more openly and loudly than before. The view that men are all portrayed as potential rapists by feminists is something that's widespread among MRAs and this issue is particularly revealing of their hypocrisy.

MRAs rally against the way that men are painted as predators (to the extent that they're refusing to have sex full stop) with particular concern for false rape allegations, and the impact these can have on the life of the accused; yet simultaneously they think it's important to raise awareness of the male victims of rape and of the need for better support. Although they make up a small minority of victims, men too suffer sexual assaults and there are indeed fewer provisions in place for supporting them, so it's absolutely not a cause that should be dismissed.

However, there's evidence to suggest that men are even more reluctant to report being raped than women. Men are often ashamed to admit they were raped because there's a view that they should be able to defend themselves – something which further reduces their sense of masculinity. Sometimes, when the victim is straight and the attacker is another man, there can be shame about their sexuality and the attack being a 'gay experience'. It manifests itself in different ways, but it's the same mindset that prevents women from speaking out. It's also an example of how rape culture affects us regardless of gender: we live in an age when many people still find it acceptable to make 'don't drop the soap'-esque jokes about prison rape, as if a man's crimes justify his being violently sexually assaulted.

Emma Garland's story will be familiar to many: a woman who didn't report her rape because she was worried it wouldn't be considered legitimate, that the police would question why she hadn't resisted, or would point out her past intimacy with her attacker in an attempt to discredit her. When women are raped, it all too often goes unreported because they don't believe the allegations will be taken seriously or that they will be blamed for it themselves. When men are raped, it goes unreported for the exact same reasons.

There's no denying that modern attitudes to sex are, in part, to blame for some of the issues surrounding rape culture. The idea that women may be seen by men as simply phys-ical conquests is surely harmful, but it's tricky to discuss this without going too far in the opposite direction and coming off as what some might call prudish. When (mostly older) people talk about a more innocent time when 'gentlemen' existed and

women were treated politely, it does admittedly sound prefer-
able to boozed-up lads looking for minge (hard to imagine your
grandpa on the lash in Magaluf, isn't it?), but these memories
are rose-tinted and, to some degree, dangerously ignorant. Yes,
there are some shitty aspects to our attitudes about sex in the
21st century and of course it would be great if we could lose
the more degrading bits of our behaviour, but in reality the only
thing majorly different from 50 years ago is that today we're
more open. And though sometimes that can suck, it's improving
a lot of lives.

When we hear about a 'rape epidemic' on college campuses,
it can feel like a bleak, hopeless situation; we ask how things
have got so bad. But while it is indeed an enormous problem and
shouldn't be dismissed by any means, some of this comes down
to the fact that victims are now more comfortable reporting and
speaking out about their experiences. Rape has always existed,
but for a lot of history, anything related to sex was considered
so shameful that victims felt unable to even admit it had happened. Think about the stigma attached to single mothers, once
so strong that society deemed it better to take a baby from its
parent than accept that a woman had sex outside of marriage.
It's important to remember this, because while some things
have improved, it is shame and stigma that continue to prevent
victims of rape speaking out: fearful that they won't be believed,
or will themselves be blamed.

It's often said that humans are among the only animals that
have sex for pleasure, and although this has been disputed by

some scholars, we are surely the only animals who have been able to separate it entirely from its biological purpose through the invention of contraception – so in this respect it's a uniquely human experience. It's certainly one of mankind's most universal interests and you'd struggle to find anything with as much cross-culture popularity as a good shag; it's got a fanbase Adele could only dream of, and *everyone* apparently loves her. Widely available and affordable contraception didn't arrive until very recently, and it was arguably our insatiable appetite for fucking which allowed us to thrive and grow to become the gargantuan population we are today: parents would continue to indulge, despite knowing they couldn't afford more children, simply because it felt so good. Face it: if pandas were as horny as humans there's no way they'd be quite so endangered.

Long before we spent our weekends binge-watching *House of Cards* on Netflix, long before we were burying our noses deep in Dickens by candlelight, long before even religion or music or art came to define the human race, we were bumping uglies, making the beast with two backs, copulating madly and so and on so forth. And long after all those things are dead and forgotten, we will continue to derive pleasure from sex.

Now, we're coming out of a brief period of repression and shame. Attitudes to sex are becoming more open, as they rightly should. It surrounds our every move, to the point where we barely blink an eye at what would once have caused outrage; it's been normalised, and we're comfortable talking about it without embarrassment. For some, this is a sign that society is over-sexualised, that this in itself is responsible for many ills and that 'loose morals' are to blame for rape culture et al.

I do think there are valid points to be made about the effects of online pornography but I disagree that censorship is the answer, nor is porn the cause of our sexual desire rather than, overwhelmingly, a symptom of it. My point in the previous paragraphs was that we, as a species, are no more interested in sex than we've ever been, and that the only thing that's changed in modernity is our honesty.

This has, however, presented some serious problems, and nowhere is this more evident than in discussion of masculinity and young men. As religious participation has waned and a lot of countries have adopted more liberal attitudes, we've seen the erosion of certain values which were essentially compulsory just a few decades ago. Sex before marriage was once deemed one of the worst sins you could commit and it had no place in civilised society, but in a relatively short span of time it has become not just acceptable, but the norm for youth, and while I've met some young people who continue to abstain for religious reasons, I know plenty more who consider premarital sex totally compatible with their faith. Although for the most part this is great, it's bred an unfortunate side effect of sex being treated almost as a commodity, which has resulted in the development of a peer pressure which was previously absent. Our basic sexual desire as humans has always been present, but for young people today there's the added weight of social conformity to carry on top of that, and it's from here that a lot of harmful behaviour stems.

In case you zoned out and failed to take in every word up to this point, here's a quick recap: men, like women, have always wanted sex. Sure, there are some exceptions, but I'd like to think we can all agree that, as a broad statement, 'men like sex', is fairly safe. In the past, marriage was the only acceptable route to sex, so couples would settle down, often when they were very young, in order to bang each other's brains out without fear of reprisal from God or being ostracised from society. What went on in the bedroom tended to be a private matter because these things weren't generally considered appropriate for conversation. There were plenty of ways in which this arrangement was horrendously damaging (which I'll get to in a moment), but unlike today there were no expectations for couples to be having sex or for sex to be linked to their social status (quite the opposite, in fact). A lot has changed. However smart you are or however much you try not to play the game, for young people, particularly men, there is an undeniable link between sexual activity and social status. People no longer just want to have sex for the act itself, they want to have sex in order to be accepted and admired among their peers, so the pressure is far more intense than it used to be. For better or worse, these attitudes are inevitable: it's how we react to them that's important now.

When we hear that children start watching porn at younger and younger ages, it's easy to believe this is proof of such material becoming normalised in society – and to an extent, that's true. Outside of hardcore pornography, sexual imagery is very much a part of the mainstream media today, and while we don't necessarily know the long-term effects of this on young minds, it is a fact of modern life that by this point we cannot change. Often, the reaction is to restrict access to the more explicit content in order to protect kids, and this has had immense support in recent years with movements calling for internet service providers to block all 'adult' sites as default, and only allow adults to view them if they opt-in. It's an understandable quick-fix solution, but one which entirely ignores the bigger issue: why are children attempting to access this material in the first place? The answer, a lot of the time, is simply *curiosity*. Sex education is still notoriously poor, and provides little detail about the act of sex itself outside of a biological context. This is something that porn can offer, at least on a superficial level. For kids approaching an age where sex is an actual possibility, porn can become a guidebook of sorts, because sex education *definitely* doesn't cover how to have satisfying sex. Back in the days when your wedding night was the first time that either partner had been intimate with another person, sex would be something you explored and learned about together. Today, there seems to be a lot more pressure to be well-versed long before you lose your virginity, because it is unlikely to be your partner's first time – and there's a worry that if you're inexperienced, other people are going to hear about it.

Education of any kind is the key to solving most of these problems, and it's *vital* we address various issues – most importantly consent – in the curriculum. But we shouldn't just rely on schools to teach young people about matters that have such profound consequences on the lives of others, and each of us has a part to play in our private lives. No one should ever be blamed for rape except rapists, but we have to accept that certain actions and attitudes we perpetuate contribute to a dangerous culture, however innocent our intentions may be. We've got to stop linking anyone's worth to their genitals or sex life, no matter how shitty a human they are, because it just allows the idea that sex = masculinity to continue.

Above all, young males need to hear about sex, rape, and consent from other men. We've already established that more openness and talking within male relationships is a good thing, the benefits of which I've largely focused on up to this point as being related to personal mental health and well-being, but now we must look at how better communication between men can bring positive changes far beyond ourselves. If fathers could get over their awkwardness and learn to talk to their sons about sex in more depth than the simple 'don't forget to use protection!' injunction, that would be ideal, or if that's not an option then maybe an older brother or other male role model could step up to the task. The earlier the better, as far as I'm concerned, but we can't just leave it at that and wait for things to hopefully improve in the future. The biggest change has to happen now, and in order for this to happen, we've got to start talking to our friends.

For fairly obvious reasons, ideas such as teaching consent are closely associated with feminism, and unfortunately there can be a tendency among some men to roll their eyes at anything feminism-related. What that means is that sensible and relatively uncontroversial thoughts are often ignored or actively opposed by people who would probably be on board were they not being presented as 'a feminist thing'. Although I suspect that most of the men reading this book are relatively supportive of feminism, there may be a few who are not so into it, and I address this question to you:

Would you be friends with a known rapist?

If not, then it's your responsibility to make sure that your friends understand all the ins and outs of consent. I get how male friendships can work, and I know that that's easier said than done. Maybe they'll rip you apart, mock you mercilessly, you might never hear the end of it. Hell, if you're super-unlucky it might genuinely destroy your relationship with them – though if you end up losing friends as a result of trying to do good, you probably shouldn't have been hanging out with them in the first place. It doesn't have to be a holier-than-thou speech or an hour long PowerPoint presentation, just a gentle word here and there when it feels appropriate – or simply any time the subject arises – and above all, calling them out on their shit as it happens. And if you're still worried about what'll happen to you if you do end up saying something, and how that'll make you feel, I'd like to remind you of a point I made earlier:

A lot of rapists don't know they're rapists.

If you would not be friends with someone you *knew* was a rapist, then I can assume you would not be friends with *any* rapist if you could somehow avoid it.

If you would not be friends with any rapist, but refuse to educate your friends on what rape is, then I have bad news: though you might not know it yet, and they might not know it yet, there's every chance you already are.

We Need To Talk:
What We Can Do To Change

A s I write this at the beginning of 2016, I am struck by what an important year 2015 was, and this one will also prove to be, for men and manhood. Discussion of masculinity is somewhat *en vogue*, people of all backgrounds are getting involved, and we are being exposed to fascinating new ideas and different takes on the subject on a daily basis. Such are the limitations of physical, print media – and my own tired brain – there will undoubtedly be glaring omissions or sections that already seem out of date by publication. Unlike, say, a history book, in which the major events of the subject have already taken place, gender – and our perception of it – is constantly evolving. In the last five years alone we've seen a huge shift in awareness of trans issues; equal marriage has arrived in much of the western world; feminism has gained widespread support, including from people who not long ago would have shuddered at the mere mention of the f-word. Who knows what progress will be made in another decade?

Consequently, I have tried to keep the book focused on what I think are a handful of major, enduring issues facing modern masculinity. It's certainly not a comprehensive work, but rather one that's intended as an introduction to this subject, written with you, the reader, in mind. The reason I was given this extraordinary opportunity to write a book in the first place came from the fact my initial VICE piece managed to engage so many people's interest in a complex subject through its simplicity and light tone. I wanted this to be an extension of that because, above all, I would like readers to get to the end and not give up from boredom halfway through. I kept the academic references to a minimum and avoided going into too much detail wherever possible. If you made it this far and want to know more, now's the time to check out the meatier stuff.

I don't know who you are or why you decided to read MAN UP and have no way of knowing yet how well the book will sell or in what demographics it will be most popular; I can only make assumptions. There is, however, a very good chance I'm preaching to the choir, or the converted, or whoever your preferred group for the sake of this idiom might be. One of the major barriers we face in our fight for social and cultural progress is that the people who care the least tend to be those we need the most effort from. Invariably, they are the ones with all the power, and when all the power is yours you're often reluctant to do anything that risks you losing your place at the top. The civil rights movement fought for centuries (and continues to do so) in the name of racial equality, but it took the support of white people for them to see actual change – not because white people were their saviours, but because they were the only ones at the time with legal and political platforms. It's a similar case for gender equality: despite the progress that's been made in the last few decades, men are still in positions of significantly greater privilege than women and we're not exactly in a rush to remedy that. With that in mind, there is a part of me that suspects the men who do the most damage with their masculinity will take one look at the blurb and hurl the book as far as they physically can (which is presumably a fair distance, what with their bulging muscles and all). But another part of me feels quite differently. Maybe it's not as simple as that, maybe we're too quick to write people off and make unfair assumptions.

Since I started writing this book, there's a phrase I've seen thrown around regularly by all sorts of people: *the patriarchy hurts men too*. Its use is sometimes controversial, not especially because of what it says, but because of what it doesn't say. Some people believe it undermines or trivialises the true power of the patriarchy, that it diverts attention away from women – who are undeniably its biggest victims – and towards men, as if to say 'you shouldn't care about this because it affects women, but because it affects you'. And yes, I agree that we have a problem when the only way people can be persuaded to give a shit about something that's harming their fellow humans on a massive scale is if they personally are affected by it too, but unfortunately that's just in a lot of people's nature. Around the 2015 UK general election, much was made of the 'shy Tories' phenomenon, in which the Conservatives consistently achieved better results than opinion polls predicted, something attributed to people being too ashamed to admit they were going to vote Tory. Why was this specific to the Tories? Because they have a reputation as the rich man's party; selfish, elitist, uninterested in helping those worse off than themselves. The existence of shy Tories suggests people are well aware the Conservatives are not the best party for the majority of Britons but vote for them anyway in the hope they, as individuals, will be better off. While I totally understand being angry or frustrated that some people only start paying attention to social injustice when it concerns them directly, it's unfortunately inevitable that this will be the case. And as far as I'm concerned, doing the right thing for the wrong reasons is a lot more helpful than doing nothing. So let's return to that phrase.

The patriarchy hurts men too.

If progress is to be made, we have to accept this fact unconditionally. It's possibly the most important weapon we have with which to fight toxic masculinity, because it's the one thing that will reach the men we need on our side more than anybody else. It's one of the reasons I got to write this thing in the first place, and it's why I think I'm wrong to assume the only people reading this went into it ready to agree with everything I say. When VICE published *A Stiff Upper Lip Is Killing British Men*, a lot of the praise it drew was from feminists – in fact it was Laurie Penny, one of the most prominent feminist writers today, who encouraged me to write the book – and though I was overwhelmingly grateful for their support, it wasn't entirely surprising. What I had not anticipated was the sheer volume of comments and messages I received from men thanking me for my honesty, calling me brave, saying how happy they were someone had finally put their thoughts into words. These weren't your liberal-arts, lefty, London-media-clique, Twitter-echo-chamber, twenty-something, social-justice types (hello there) but ordinary men with ordinary jobs and ordinary lives; guys, dudes, blokes, lads. I even saw it posted by a handful of Men's Rights Activists who, amusingly, said it was proof that feminism had gone too far. Regardless of their motives, what united all these people was their opposition to a system that harms men. Toxic masculinity affects us all, but if our lives are to improve we need to give its worst perpetrators incentive to change. Acknowledging that the patriarchy hurts men is a good first step.

What's in it for us?

Gender equality is often discussed in terms of the benefits it brings women, which for some men should be enough to make them care. However, as I just touched upon, some men may need to be given personal incentive before they make any changes to their behaviour, and that's cool, I get it, looking out for number one et cetera. Men do stand to gain a lot from a more equal society, and often the benefits are reciprocal. A few examples include:

Better relationships – the chance to love and be loved by someone who is actually willing to work with you and be the partner you want and need, to support you and coach you through the hard times.

Fatherhood – obviously men haven't exactly struggled with becoming dads in the most literal sense, but in the modern world we're becoming a lot more aware of the joy that hands-on parenting can bring. Issues such as unequal statutory paternity leave and divorce courts favouring mothers in custody battles have been campaigned against for a while now, but we're not going to see full-on progress made in this world unless other gender inequalities are addressed first.

Longer lives – this one's fairly self explanatory isn't it?

Happiness – the most important one of all. Gender inequality is responsible for so many ills, and for men the most serious of these is the toll it takes on our mental wellbeing and all-round contentedness. Men are crushed under the weight of the expectations society lays on them, forbidden from becoming emotionally mature and taught to repress any negative thoughts, with destructive consequences. Gender equality would mean an end in sight for the deadliest symptom of toxic masculinity.

So what should we do then?

When I set out to write MAN UP, long before I'd put any words on the page I had a handful of ideas about what I wanted it to be. It was never going to be a dry, academic text and work its way into medical reference libraries because I'm not, by my nature, an academic ('No shit,' I hear you say). More importantly, academic books are rarely read by anyone other than academics, and I wanted something ordinary people would be tempted to pick up.

   The most ambitious of my aims was a desire to offer practical solutions, to help people in whatever way I could to address their problems and start to grow. You've probably noticed that I had regular conflicts with myself throughout the book over the best way to approach these issues, and this is exactly why. It's easy enough to explore several theories and argue about the benefits and downsides of each, but when they so often contradict one another it's not much use to anyone who actually wants to change.

Two of the best-known campaigns against male suicide in Britain were spearheaded by the Samaritans and CALM, respectively. The Samaritans, using images of masculine characters talking about their struggles with mental health, wanted to spread the message that it's not emasculating to ask for help and that 'real' men got depressed too; CALM partnered with Lynx, a company notorious for ads that reinforce stereotypes of masculinity, in order to hit a broader audience. In terms of achieving their aim to reduce male suicide, this tactic was smart and effective, essentially turning toxic masculinity in on itself in order to save lives. If this is what you must do to prevent those most at risk from taking their own lives – and evidence suggests it is – then it's absolutely vital as a short-term solution. Suicide is the most profoundly devastating concern of toxic masculinity right now, and, in my opinion, the issue that requires the most immediate action.

The very existence of these campaigns shows how damaging toxic masculinity is, and I'm guessing you're not going to find anyone involved in them who doesn't think we need to take significant steps towards addressing this on a long term basis. But this is when things get a lot more complicated. We can't tackle this in the long term until we move away from our rigid ideas of what masculinity is; while men still feel these are imposed upon them, and are what is expected of them, it's going to result in toxic behaviour.

This is a dilemma that's almost inevitable within any social movement as support grows. If an individual or group does the right thing for the wrong reasons, or the right thing in the wrong way, is it still the right thing? I didn't anticipate me bringing up Taylor Swift's feminism in this book, but I recently witnessed a debate about this between two women which proved surprisingly relevant to this situation. One side centred on Swift's rich, white, straight woman brand of feminism, and argued that because of her massive platform, she was doing more harm than good by preaching her love for something that excludes less privileged women. The other, while in agreement that there were problems with this, said it was a good thing overall because it started a conversation (particularly amongst younger women and girls) and taught them feminism didn't have to be a dirty word. Above all, it might encourage them to learn more, and in turn reject the problematic elements of what initially sparked their interest. And I have to say, I agree.

It's difficult to change anything that's even remotely political, because no matter how much you want something or think it's necessary, there will always be people who oppose you. What makes it even harder is that people on your own side will disagree as to the best course of action, and humans can be so set in their principles that compromise is viewed as failure. Ambition is a wonderful thing, but too much of it can ultimately prove damaging in practice.

Returning briefly to those campaigns by the Samaritans and CALM, when I consider the bigger picture and how they impact upon a more long-term outlook, I can't in good conscience support them. However, if the alternative at this point in time means that more men will take their own lives, that's obviously far, far worse. If we're to truly make things better for future generations, we have to completely change the way we think about gender and stop imposing arbitrary values on each other. I am more certain of this than anything, but the fact is that right now we are dealing with what is effectively an epidemic of male suicide and must use every resource we have to bring those numbers down, even if it seems counterintuitive in the long term. It might not be perfect, but I do believe it's achiev- able: and if men can first see that it's not emasculating to open up or ask for help, they're likely to be more receptive to even bigger ideas than this. That's not to say that in the meantime we should ignore the long term goals, or shy away from calling out campaigns and trying to improve things – Lynx may reach a lot of men, but I'm sure there are plenty of other brands capable of doing this who don't have the same history of dodgy advertising. But we can only adhere to our idealistic views for so long before we have to accept that nothing is changing, and that imperfect progress is better than no progress at all.

All of us have a part to play but none more than men, *obviously*. First things first, we have to fix ourselves. We have to learn to be comfortable in who we are, inside and out. We have to change the way we deal with our problems, and realise that opening up to those we love and trust will not emasculate us but empower us. We have to stop and think critically about what masculinity even is, and question everything we do in its name, ask what good this can bring besides boosting our own fra- gile egos. We have to learn to treat women and LGBT people properly, and fight for their causes – if not out of sheer human decency and a desire to aid others, then for the purely selfish reasons that their liberation will serve us well too.

Then we have to deal with other men. Our male friends and family members. We have to reach out to them when we suspect they're in need, we have to ensure they know they can talk without fear of judgment or having their masculinity questioned. We have to educate them. We have to discourage the worst of their toxic behaviours, we have to teach them about consent and rape culture and make it known that certain things, however lighthearted their intentions, are not at all okay.

Everyone else has to chip in too. We all have to stop assigning value to sexuality or physical beauty – regardless of who the subject is – and perpetuating the idea that masculinity can come from something out of the beholder's control. We have to stop the culture that tells men masculinity is the most important thing in the world, more so than even their lives. We have to stop gendering arbitrary products or saying things like 'boys don't cry', because if we don't, nothing's ever going to change.

The idea that our modern perception of masculinity is harmful is something agreed upon by people from across the spectrum. When my first article for VICE was published in 2014, it received, as I said before, vocal support from feminists as well as men's rights activists. That such opposite viewpoints felt themselves represented proved that there is a consensus that masculinity is a major cause of problems – even if different groups think that this is for seemingly very different reasons. 'Masculinity in crisis' has been a point of discussion for decades, and in this context usually refers to the effects of men feeling increasingly redundant in a world moving towards greater gender equality, and women taking roles traditionally reserved for men. Many proponents of the 'masculinity in crisis' theory – at least in the Men's Rights camp – believe that the solution to men's problems lies in reclaiming what was ours and teaches that feminism is the enemy: after all, feminism has primarily fought to prove that women are capable of doing anything men can. But just take a moment to consider how much this reveals about the regressive reaction of men.

We feel threatened by women achieving historically masculine feats, but what is striking is that they do so without abandoning important and desirable feminine qualities. Women are still much more emotionally developed and, while admittedly not 100% scientifically provable, I would posit that they are able to deal with potentially worrying matters in a more open and thus healthier manner than men. As long as men embrace a stiff upper lip, they will continue to be plagued by their own emotional shortcomings and become an objectively inferior gender. Acceptance of and support for feminism is only going to grow, and to believe masculinity can only be saved by opposing this is to fight a losing battle. If men are to avoid redundancy, we must instead look to feminism and ask what we can learn from women if we are to better ourselves. Women have already proven they are capable of anything men can do; men must now prove they are capable of anything women can do.

Above all else, we have to realise that the qualities we perceive as integral to masculinity are not fixed. Most of the commonly accepted qualities that we consider specific to one gender date back centuries or even millennia and originally served purposes that simply aren't relevant today, because of technological advancements and how vastly our gender roles have changed in such a short space of time. Behavioural attributes such as aggression, or philosophical concepts like courage, were vital for hunter-gatherer men in order to successfully provide for or defend their families. They continued to be desirable traits in, for just one example, soldiers, right up until the easing of restrictions on women in the military. In post-industrial society, biological factors such as physical strength are no longer an asset in most fields of employment; advances in medical science, particularly in areas of reproductive study, mean there is little need for women to seek out virile or genetically superior partners to start a family; even very modern sociological constructions of masculinity, such as those related to financial success, are becoming less relevant (albeit rather slowly) as more women begin to occupy top jobs and accumulate greater personal wealth.

When these are the qualities by which we define masculinity, then yes, it is indeed in crisis; doomed, in fact. However, the historical significance of these qualities was a direct result of distinct gender roles, which in turn were created by biological factors that are now no longer relevant. Humans are unique in their constant thirst for knowledge and progression, but such growth is only made possible by cooperation. You know those god-awful motivational posters that spell out 'TEAM' with the words 'Together Everyone Achieves More'? Sure, they're in the top five crimes against humanity, but the message is true. For most of our existence, gender roles were an unavoidable necessity for the advancement of the human race, so the idealistic traits of a social construct like masculinity grew from something that began as being genuinely beneficial to the species. To put it simply, when men and women each had one clearly defined set of roles in order to further human development with little crossover between the two, it made sense for men to be as manly as they could, and vice-versa. Today, the benefits of such masculinity are negligible.

Masculinity isn't in crisis, it's just confused

The qualities we deem to be masculine can absolutely be admired, but in our pursuit of these we all too often erase their true meaning and end up chasing idealised, superficial versions. But there are no shortcuts, and you cannot simply act masculine – it's a complex state that requires far more balance and nuance than we often accept. Strength, courage, assertiveness can all be wonderful characteristics but only in the right hands, and there is much more to masculinity than what we see on the surface. If you're trying to achieve an idealised state of masculinity then you've already failed at your goal; true masculinity is something you must earn by using your gender in a way that benefits everyone.

There is a belief amongst a lot of men that hypermasculinity will make them more attractive to women, but their fundamental idea of what constitutes masculinity is deeply confused. Their attitudes towards women as a result can often be appalling (and, ironically, unattractive) and while certain masculine qualities can indeed be attractive, a lot of men unfortunately have no understanding of the intricacies of this behaviour or the appropriate contexts in which it's acceptable. They attempt to appear confident and instead come off as arrogant, try to be assertive but just sound rude. They lack any real self-awareness; their efforts to seem masculine are clearly founded on an arbitrary list. And vitally, they fail to grasp that *masculinity is not the opposite of femininity.*

Beyond all else, in our efforts to appear masculine we seem to set aside all common sense and thus push these to the extreme. We're told it's not sexy to be overly emotional and so we bottle up everything in an attempt to avoid this, but in reality this boils down to 'maybe don't come on like a drunk high school poet on a first date' not, 'try to come across as robotic as possible and don't admit to ever feeling anything'.

Equality benefits us all, and division does only harm. Through feminism, women have proven to the sexists that they can do anything men can do, and, largely thanks to feminism, their lives in secular western countries are now better than at any point in history. Now it's time for men to prove they can do anything women can do. Our dicks won't fall off, football won't cease to exist, and no one's going to force you to waltz around in a frilly dress and high heels – but nor will women judge you if that's what you want to do. We can still leave 'the missus' for the night and go to the pub with 'the lads', and chat whatever shit we like, and after all that, just maybe, at our lowest we'll no longer suffer in silence, and with the help of each other we'll get through the darkest hours and emerge on the other side, victorious. It would not be an end to masculinity, but a beginning.

And it wouldn't be quite as fucking cheesy as that.

Acknowledgements

I'm indebted to many people for their roles in making this book a reality, but none more so than Juliet Pickering at Blake Friedmann, the finest agent you could ask for. Enormous thanks also to Laurie Penny, who told me I should write this damn book in the first place; Tom Webber at Icon Books for the frankly wild risk he took on this barely-known writer and his tireless efforts as an editor; and Jamie Clifton at VICE UK for commissioning the piece that sparked all of this off. I'm also unbelievably grateful for the hard work of Hattie Grünewald, Claire Maxwell, Andrew Furlow, Stevie Finegan, Steve White and all at Icon.

For their eloquent and insightful interviews, endless praise for: Megan Tucker, Jonny Sharples, Geoff Lamb, Josh Huddleston, Christina Bentley, Huw Oliver, Ryan Atkins, Séan Faye and Emily Reynolds.

For general friendship, moral support, inspiration, unsolicited plugging of my work or having had an otherwise unspecified impact on this book (the most coveted position): Kris Lavin, Jess Partridge, Dave Rowlinson, Lewis Moulds, Emma Garland, Hannah Ewens, Leo May, Richard Brett, Jake Walker, Erin

Bradshaw, Richard Crook, Rebecca Suner, Marie Le Conte, Duncan Vicat-Brown, Merlin Jobst, Rachael Krishna, Caroline Hatwell, Mollie Goodfellow, Joel Golby, Eleanor Penny, Keith Morris, Gina Pantone-Urwin, Paul Widdowfield, the Terpstras, Us Kids Know, the employees of the Buffalo Bar, the residents of the Jack Beard's Pub in Islington 2011–2012, and the staff at Mountfields Lodge Primary School and the institutions formerly known as Woodbrook Vale High School and Rawlins Community College.

And finally, special thanks to my family – especially Mum, Sarah and Tom, without whom none of this would have happened; Alison, for putting up with and loving me; and Dad, for obvious reasons.

Dedicated to Richard and Alf

References

1. NHS UK (20th January 2014) 'Five health symptoms men shouldn't ignore' http://www.nhs.uk/Livewell/men1839/Pages/Menshealthweek.aspx
2. Poverty (retrieved May 2015) 'Premature death' http://www.poverty.org .uk/60/index.shtml
3. Cancer Research UK (22nd April 2014) 'Skin cancer incidence statistics) http://www.cancerresearchuk.org/cancer-info/cancerstats/types/skin/ incidence/uk-skin-cancer-incidence-statistics
4. Anna Hodgekiss, *Daily Mail* (19th February 2014) 'Men are now THREE times more likely to commit suicide than women - and is the recession to blame?' http://www.dailymail.co.uk/health/article-2562871/Men-THREE -times-likely-commit-suicide-women-recession-blame.html
5. Samaritans (September 2012) 'Men, Suicide and Society: Why disadvantaged men in mid-life die by suicide' http://www.samaritans.org/ sites/default/files/kcfinder/files/Men%20and%20Suicide%20Research %20Report%20210912.pdf
6. VICE UK, (17th October 2014) http://www.vice.com/en_uk/read/a-stiff -upper-lip-is-killing-british-men-344
7. http://www.forbes.com/sites/kerryadolan/2015/03/02/inside-the-2015 -forbes-billionaires-list-facts-and-figures/#2715e4857a0b1852125c6cec
8. http://www.telegraph.co.uk/news/uknews/11360819/Average-cost-of -raising-a-child-in-UK-230000.html
9. http://www.thisismoney.co.uk/money/mortgageshome/article-2649768/ Potential-homebuyers-undercook-cost-monthly-mortgage-payments.html
10. http://www.bbc.co.uk/history/british/britain_wwone/pals_01.shtml
11. http://www.dailymail.co.uk/news/article-1222381/How-Nick-Griffin-left -Jack-Straw-speechless-pathetic-attack-fathers-wartime-jail-spell.html
12. http://www.theguardian.com/theobserver/2005/jan/23/features.review7
13. http://www.theguardian.com/society/2015/feb/19/number-of-suicides -uk-increases-2013-male-rate-highest-2001

14. http://www.theguardian.com/society/2013/may/22/women-men-mental
    -illness-study
15. 'Accounting For Taste', Nicola Twilley, p53, *The New Yorker*
    (2nd November 2015)
16. Average number between 2005 and 2009 for male car drivers was 5,781;
    for female car drivers it was 2,742. https://www.gov.uk/government/
    uploads/system/uploads/attachment_data/file/467465/rrcgb-2014.pdf
17. Sarah Whyte, *Sydney Morning Herald* (11th January 2014) 'Road
    safety ad shows size does matter when engaging young male egos'
    http://www.smh.com.au/nsw/road-safety-ad-shows-size-does-matter
    -when-engaging-young-male-egos-20140110-30mjz.html
18. *The Telegraph* (21st September 2014) 'Turkey combats hooligan problem
    by banning men and letting 41,000 women in for free' http://www
    .telegraph.co.uk/sport/football/8778310/Turkey-combats-hooligan
    -problem-by-banning-men-and-letting-41000-women-in-for-free.html
19. London in Stereo (October 2014) http://issuu.com/londoninstereo/docs/
    october2014/60
20. Jack Millner, *Daily Mail* (11th December 2014) 'It's official – men
    are idiots! Analysis of the Darwin Awards for stupid deaths reveals
    the 'winners' are overwhelmingly male' http://www.dailymail.co.uk/
    sciencetech/article-2870374/Darwin-Awards-winners-overwhelmingly
    -male-analysis-reveals.html
21. https://www.gov.uk/government/news/military-recognised-in
    -stonewalls-top-100
22. http://www.theguardian.com/commentisfree/2014/sep/18/52-percent
    -people-playing-games-women-industry-doesnt-know
23. http://www.cnn.com/2015/07/01/health/ptsd-vets-and-fireworks-irpt/
24. http://www.theguardian.com/commentisfree/2015/dec/18/republicans
    -are-so-bullish-on-war-that-30-percent-would-bomb-a-fictional-country
25. http://www.theatlantic.com/national/archive/2014/05/elliot-rodger-and
    -poisonous-ideals-of-masculinity/371588/
26. www.theguardian.com/lifeandstyle/2015/jan/18/are-more-men-getting
    -eating-disorders
27. http://www.telegraph.co.uk/women/sex/11820710/Women-more-likely
    -to-be-bisexual-study-finds.html
28. http://www.independent.co.uk/life-style/health-and-families/features/
    protein-supplements-are-generating-huge-profits-but-do-they-really
    -help-you-slim-10311581.html
29. http://www.bbc.co.uk/news/magazine-22753620
30. https://twitter.com/NoEmployer/status/391302785784102912
31. http://nypost.com/2015/03/03/man-arrested-in-brutal-beating-of
    -transgender-woman/
32. http://www.rollingstone.com/culture/news/the-transgender-crucible
    -20140730

33. http://time.com/134152/the-toxic-appeal-of-the-mens-rights-movement/
34. http://jezebel.com/5967923/fuck-you-mras
35. Laurie Penny, *Unspeakable Things: Sex, Lies and Revolution*, Bloomsbury (2014)
36. http://www.gq.com/story/michael-fassbender-gq-june-2012-interview
37. 26th November 2015 http://www.theguardian.com/commentisfree/2015/nov/26/wanker-porn-epidemic-editor-loaded-sex-consent
38. 4th December 2015 https://medium.com/@emmaggarland/defining-absence-a49eabe59210#.un04wz44k
39. Emilie Buchwald, *Transforming a Rape Culture*, Milkweed Editions (1993)
40. 9th December 2014 http://www.newsweek.com/campus-rapists-and-semantics-297463
41. 6th March 2015 http://www.independent.co.uk/news/uk/crime/teenager-ben-moynihan-sentenced-to-21-years-for-attempted-murder-of-three-women-because-he-could-not-10091277.html
42. 15th November 2015 http://www.thesundaytimes.co.uk/sto/Magazine/article1629220.ece
43. 13th March 2013 http://www.theguardian.com/society/2013/mar/13/rape-investigations-belief-false-accusations